# EMERGING
## FROM
# DARKNESS

# EMERGING FROM DARKNESS

## A SPIRITUAL MEMOIR AND GUIDE BACK TO THE LIGHT

## BRIANNA LADAPO

FOREWORD BY **CHRISTIANE NORTHRUP, MD**

AFTERWORD BY **CHRISTOPHER LEE MAHER**

Skyhorse Publishing

Skyhorse Publishing books may be purchased in bulk at special discounts
for sales promotion, corporate gifts, fund-raising, or educational purposes.
Special editions can also be created to specifications. For details, contact the
Special Sales Department, Skyhorse Publishing, 307 West 36th Street,
11th Floor, New York, NY 10018 or info@skyhorsepublishing.com.

Skyhorse® and Skyhorse Publishing® are registered trademarks of Skyhorse
Publishing, Inc.®, a Delaware corporation.

Visit our website at www.skyhorsepublishing.com.

10 9 8 7 6 5 4 3 2 1

Library of Congress Cataloging-in-Publication Data is available on file.

Cover design by Kai Texel
Cover photo courtesy of Getty Images

Print ISBN: 978–1-5107–7784-2
Ebook ISBN: 978–1-5107–7838-2

Printed in the United States of America

# DEDICATION

To my extraordinary husband Joe. You are my love, my light, and my king, and you possess the purest and most courageous heart I have ever known. Thank you for always seeing the divine in me, even when I did not see it myself.

To our sons, Eric, Jack, and Max. You beautiful angels light up the earth, and you light up my heart. I am honored to be your mama.

And to my soul tribe, my dearest friends, who have stood strong with me and loved me through everything. You know who you are.

I love you all and am forever grateful that we get to take this remarkable journey together.

# CONTENTS

# FOREWORD
## CHRISTIANE NORTHRUP, MD

THE MOMENT I FIRST spoke with Brianna Ladapo in a phone conversation, I felt as though I were talking to a member of my innermost circle. We were on the same page about health, spirituality, and the ultimate ascension of humanity from the tyranny that has gripped the globe since the onset of the COVID debacle. But of course, as most of us now know, this tyranny has been present on some level for centuries before COVID; the virus was merely the final act in a long strategy meant to enslave humanity. The good news is that each and every one of us chose to be here on planet Earth at this time, which shamanic astrologer Daniel Giamario calls "The Turning of the Ages." And despite how bad it has been for so many, it's important to know that we each have the ability—once tapped—to turn things around and change them for the better. That is the mission of this book: to stare down the abuse in your own life, tell the truth about it, and then do what is necessary to end it in your own lineage.

Please note that this kind of inner work rarely includes a Hollywood ending in which the family who abused you gathers together in love and forgiveness. This almost never happens, and it would serve all of us to assume that it won't. You can love your abusers from a distance without expecting them to change, as the only person you can change is yourself. The cancel culture of COVID—in which families turned on each other over their testing, vaccination, or mask status—illustrates perfectly how easy it is for many humans to reject and condemn their loved ones rather than attempt to bridge their differences through communication and personal growth. (And yes, the extensive gaslighting by global predators, which has been astounding to witness, has strained most people's ability to see clearly.)

I have spent a lifetime endeavoring to help women, children, and their families live healthy, joyful lives—starting with helping women and men prepare for conception and pregnancy. My work has always been right up there at the very headwaters of our health, and the springs of wisdom that create those headwaters flow directly to us from our parents, grandparents, great-grandparents, and ancestry even further back—along with all the generational trauma they have accumulated. So, for example, when a mother tells her pregnant daughter, "Now you'll see how I suffered with you," that clearly reveals a legacy of pain that needs to be transformed. I have written some very long books with endless examples of this phenomenon.

Every human alive on this planet has a story within his or her DNA that not only speaks of our legacies of pain and suffering, but which also provides massive clues about what our souls chose to transform when we chose to be born here on Earth. As painful and unfair as it may look from a human perspective, this was a soul choice. If you accept this, your life will be a whole lot easier.

As it turns out, pregnancy and birth present unique biological opportunities to upgrade our legacies—but you don't have to have a baby in order to do the hard work of healing the trauma in your lineage. You can start right now by reading this book and applying the incredible wisdom here in your own life. In my decades of practice, I have repeatedly seen how crucial it is to take personal responsibility for upgrading our familial legacies of pain. We are not responsible for what happened to us as innocent children, or for what happened to our ancestors in their childhoods, but to change that legacy, we must be willing—with God's help—to take responsibility for doing the work of transformation. Otherwise, we just become willing players in our family's chain of pain. No one manifests his or her true power and potential without first acknowledging their family histories and their personal legacies—that is the first and most crucial step to healing. There is no diet, no exercise regimen, no meditation technique, no ashram, no church, no book, and no program—no matter how brilliant and well thought out—that will free you from your personal demons and those you inherited through your family. You have to take responsibility for your own healing. We are endlessly taught that we are powerless victims, and we use our pain as an excuse, thus losing the opportunity for true health and transformation. Healing is very hard work; schoolroom Earth is not for the weak.

That is why very few people are willing to do the work so brilliantly laid out here, and that is one of the reasons I was so taken with this memoir. It is said that the blood of the wound contains the cure, and that is the truth. We have much to learn from Brianna Ladapo's treacherous—and ultimately triumphant—journey. Take strength from her story and the way in which she overcame her origins. Nothing is harder . . . but nothing is more rewarding. Brianna Ladapo, I commend you. If I could, I would make you a Knight of the House of Brilliant Health and Healing. Well done, my soul sister. Well done.

# AUTHOR'S NOTE

THIS BOOK IS AN honest recounting of my personal journey from my perspective, shared expressly for the purpose of helping anyone who may benefit from my experience. As such, it may be painful for some to read, whether because they were directly involved or because it is reflective of their own experience. However, it is not, and never will be, my intention to hurt anyone. I have learned the hard way that we must speak the truth, however painful, in order to heal from it. Without acknowledging the truth about your past, it is not possible to have an honest, joyful present or future.

This book is about the divine personal journey from the darkness into the light, and the collective journey we have undertaken as human beings incarnated on the earth plane at this spectacular moment of change to move out of the separation consciousness that keeps us locked in conflict and suffering, and into divine unity.

Though it may appear as though our world has never been darker or housed more suffering, humanity is experiencing an unprecedented awakening—and each of us has chosen to participate. We are witnessing the convergence of human understanding and divine expression that will ultimately lead to the ascension of humankind and the creation of a new world that works for everyone. But in order to create this beautiful new world, we must have the courage and clarity to leave the old one behind.

I hope this work will serve as both loving support and encouragement for all those who are suffering under the current reality, and a practical guide for ridding oneself of the manipulative, toxic programming that keeps us locked into patterns of destructive behavior and prevents us from realizing and embracing the incredible power of our true natures to create the world we want.

# EMERGING
## FROM
# DARKNESS

# CHAPTER ONE

FOR THE FIRST TWENTY years of my life, I genuinely believed that my ending up on earth was some sort of tragic mistake. I was certain that somebody in the great company of heaven had erred, perhaps hitting an incorrect key on the galactic travel log or confusing me with the soul of a mighty Gurkha, because I clearly didn't belong here.

Naturally a joyful, sensitive little creature, I found myself quite incompatible with my surroundings. Earth and the humans inhabiting it struck me as very harsh, and my most vivid early memories are of the relentless assaults on my young senses. My ears rang from the cacophony of screaming adults, roaring transportation vehicles, and explosions from the nearby military base. My eyes squinted and teared in the penetrating light from bulbs and screens. My skin burned and swelled in response to the glorious, yet unforgiving sun and wind. My tongue singed and recoiled from harsh, unfamiliar chemicals with every bite of processed food. My nose puckered and flinched from the unbearable stench of rotting garbage and noxious perfume. But oddly, no one else seemed to register these intrusions as bothersome.

We took a family vacation to Nevada when I was a child, and because my father was a big fan of the television show *Bonanza*, we visited the Ponderosa ranch near Lake Tahoe. I have two distinct memories from that day: first, learning that "sarsaparilla" was basically root beer, and second, hiding in a porta-potty, desperately trying to shield my ears while the rest of my family enjoyed the ranch's wild-west gun show. Under normal circumstances, being within twenty feet of a portable toilet would have been an unthinkable, malodorous nightmare for me, but that day, it was wildly preferable to the violent explosions and appreciative shouts taking place just outside my rancid refuge.

Prior to that day, I had never heard a weapon fired up close, and was surprised to discover that each burst of gunfire pierced my consciousness like a searing ice pick being driven mercilessly into my brain. The deafening percussion of each blast tore through me like vibrating shrapnel, rattling my senses. Behind my tightly closed eyes, I saw an endless reel of every soul in history who had been brutalized by firearms, with images of one savage death chasing the next—complete with detailed visions of each anguished face—and I felt the suffering of every single one. It wasn't the first time I had experienced the pain of those who passed before me, but at that point in my young life, it was the most intense. I found myself wishing the faux cowboys would kindly shoot me so I wouldn't have to feel it anymore.

But my parents and sister loved it, regaling each other with opinions and reenactments all the way back home to California. When they asked me why I had run away from the show, why I didn't want to "join in the fun" as they put it, I tried to explain to them that for me, the experience had been terribly jarring and unpleasant. I remember exactly how my father looked at me in that moment, with utter bewilderment, disappointment, and disbelief—like I couldn't possibly be related to him.

It was far from the last time he would look at me that way. Similar scenarios arose throughout my entire childhood, each one further frustrating my parents and making me feel like an alien who had veered terribly off course and crash-landed in the wrong family. Whereas they enjoyed raucous competitive events, watching nightly disasters on mainstream news, and superficial small talk with the other church families, I craved meaningful connections, solitude, and peaceful time spent in nature. I felt as though I could scarcely connect to the fading murmurs of my soul trying desperately to speak louder than the constant noise of this foreign world. Yet, everyone around me seemed unburdened by this conundrum, which baffled me.

I share none of this with the intention of disparaging my birth family. Despite our vastly different worldviews and choices, I love my parents and extended family, and acknowledge that all are products of their environment who did the best they could with the hand they were dealt, as we all do. Rather, I share this because of the critically important role this combative environment played in preparing me for the missions I have undertaken as an adult, which would not be possible had I not learned to trust myself implicitly, regardless of any and all external pressures.

As a highly sensitive child, I was always very aware of how others were feeling, and I could read their thoughts and moods as easily as I could my own. I could quite literally see the energy of other humans as colorful, swirling auras, which immediately informed me of their disposition and intentions. While beautiful golden or blue light signified a safe, benevolent being, gray, stormy energy indicated darkness and danger. I knew things about people simply by looking at them, and often mystified my parents with my ability to discern someone's family life, level of happiness at work, or history of abuse just by being in their presence.

Whenever I thought about a thing or place or person, all of my senses would collaborate to create a profound experience of that thing in my mind, and I would simultaneously smell or taste or feel it as strongly as if it were right there in front of me. When I was a child, this would often manifest in my smelling and tasting my favorite treats, usually cinnamon rolls or molasses cookies, when they were nowhere around, or smelling and feeling my beloved German shepherd, Snickers, snuggle up next to me, long after she passed away. As an adult, I am often overwhelmed by the sweet scent of roses where there are none (like in the middle of the ocean) and the smell of my long-departed great-grandfather's pipe in my own bedroom (and no, my scientifically minded friends—it is not a brain tumor).

I frequently experienced an interesting phenomenon where warm, tingly, dancing energy would come up from the earth through the bottoms of my feet, swirl up into my calves and thighs, expand into my root and sacral chakras, and fill my solar plexus and heart chakras until I felt I was going to burst. The energy felt loving, magical, and delicious, but it was also overwhelming, and clearly something that needed to find a way out of my body, but it always seemed to get stuck right in my throat chakra. It was very frustrating! Imagine having to sneeze, but with your entire mind, body, and soul. When this happened, I would close my eyes, root myself into the ground, and breathe deeply and steadily until all of that energy was released, finally exploding simultaneously out of my crown and third eye chakras in the form of big yawns, stretches, or full-body shaking. The experience is reminiscent of an orgasm, but from your soul (I eventually started calling them "soul-gasms"), and often with an even greater release, as the entirety of your being is involved. It happened very often as a child and I didn't understand it, but as I grew, I noticed that it usually occurred when I was experiencing divine truth or divine synchronicity. For example, it happened anytime I stumbled upon exactly what I needed at the very moment I needed it, discovered information that I knew, at a soul level, to be true, or met someone who turned out to be a lifelong kindred spirit. I realized that the energetic explosions indicated a deep resonance with my higher self, and I came to trust them as happy harbingers of the divine.

I had always felt a constant, deep, and profound connection to Godsource, and felt little need to look outside my own intuition for understanding or explanation of the universe. As long as I can remember, I have received communications from beings beyond this realm. Even as a young child, angels regularly spoke to me, relaying messages of comfort, hope, and safety, and I came to rely on these messages to navigate my Earth journey.

In one such instance, my mother dropped off my younger sister and me at the movie theater. As we were buying our tickets, I noticed a man watching us. His energy unnerved me (he had a swirling, dark gray aura), so we quickly went inside. After buying our snacks, we entered the near-empty theater and took seats about halfway down the length of the theater, right in the center of the row, where there was nobody around us. We enjoyed the movie in peace for about twenty minutes, at which point I was overcome with an overwhelming feeling of dread. At first, it was confusing, as there seemed to be no immediate threat . . . after all, we were just watching a kid's movie in an empty theater. Then I heard a warm, angelic voice in my consciousness say, "turn around, beloved." So I did—and there, sitting in the row directly behind us, was the man I had seen outside.

I grabbed my sister and we raced out of there. Luckily, there was a police kiosk in the strip mall where the theater was located, so we headed there and called my mom to come pick us up. I thought that was the end of it, but the next morning, the local news reported that a young girl about our age had been raped in the alley behind the theater the previous night. In my gut, I knew it was him, and I knew we had been his intended targets. My angels kept me safe that night, as they have countless times before, and do to this day.

Since I was born, I have also received constant communications in the form of visions. At first, I thought I was merely having dreams like everyone else, but I soon realized that my dreams were actually premonitions, as they kept coming true. While I did occasionally have regular old dreams, my visions were distinct because, unlike in dreams—where I would remember very little, and whatever memories I did have would start to fade the moment I woke up—I could remember every single detail of my visions and recount them perfectly years later; they never faded, and eventually, every single one of them came to pass.

Some were as benign as seeing a single image frozen in time. I recall one vision I had when I was about six years old of a huge pickup truck, painted a vivid purple with orange flames down the sides, parked at the local farmer's market we frequented. The very next day, my mother took us to that farmer's market, and what was parked right in front when we pulled up? The big purple pickup with flames on it.

Others were more intricate, and some even disturbing. One night, I had a vision of a fast food restaurant being robbed by a man with spiky blond hair. I didn't think much of it, as a few weeks went by without incident. Then one night, my mother and her friend took my sister and me for a "girl's night." We pulled into a shopping center and decided that my sister and I would go to Blockbuster to rent a movie, while my mom and her friend would go to the grocery store to get dessert, and then we would meet at the pizza place in between them to pick up dinner. In the midst of happily browsing the new releases at the video store, I was suddenly overcome with that familiar dread. I went outside and looked around, but nothing seemed amiss. However, my internal alarms kept going off. Finally, I grabbed my sister and set off to find my mother, but just as we stepped out of the Blockbuster, I saw a man with spiky blond hair rush into the pizza place with his hand in his pocket and jam the door behind him. He moved out of sight after that, but we later heard that the pizza place had been robbed at gunpoint.

I have also had countless visions of myself in various time periods and parts of the world. There was a particularly persistent vision that I had almost nightly for the first twelve years of my life, and then periodically for years after, in which I was sitting on an elevated stage, looking out through my own eyes at a grand celebration taking place in the courtyard of a magnificent temple. It was clear from the hieroglyphics on the columns surrounding me and the regalia of the soldiers guarding me that I was in ancient Egypt. There were thousands of people in the courtyard, all celebrating me and the person sitting next to me onstage, who I could strongly feel, but never see. Night after night for decades, that's where the vision ended. I never saw any more of the picture until I visited Egypt in graduate school. There, I had the honor of visiting many sacred temples and other sites of deep spiritual significance where I had many profound experiences. These experiences—which I would never have believed were possible had I not experienced them myself—catapulted me into an incredible spiritual awakening and helped me see the rest of that recurring vision, which I ultimately realized was of a particularly meaningful past life . . . but we'll revisit that later.

As a little girl, I shared these visions and experiences freely with my family. Since humans always define the world through their own experiences, I did not—in my childhood naivete—realize that my experience was unusual (and should probably have been kept to myself). However, my deeply religious family soon educated me.

# CHAPTER TWO

MY MOTHER'S SIDE OF the family was Protestant, and my father's side was Catholic: both fundamentalist, both true believers, and both thoroughly convinced that the other side was going to hell. I found myself a prisoner of war caught between the opposing sides, both of whom began vying for my allegiance to their belief systems from the day I was born.

I remember each Christmas, Easter, and birthday dependably bringing Bible wars, as various family members embraced the opportunity to slip me their version of the good word, sneak me into a children's Bible study designed to save my young soul (Psalty the Singing Songbook disturbs me to this day), or surreptitiously denigrate the efforts and teachings of the other side of my family. Their fighting was constant. If my father's side of the family let us watch *Bedknobs and*

*Broomsticks,* my mother's side would call it witchcraft and threaten us with eternal damnation. If my mother's side of the family took me to my beloved ballet classes, my father's side would insist that only a Jezebel would wear such revealing clothing (referring to my class-issued pink leotard and tights).

Neither side would ever consent to having an open, honest conversation with the other, and nobody could ever tolerate my questions about perceived inconsistencies in their beloved dogma, so they simply continued trying to persuade me with impassioned speeches and promises of heaven if I complied, all the while thrusting religious texts at me. If memory serves, I had amassed six different versions of the Bible by the time I had had as many birthdays.

Rather than making me the believer they had hoped, their incessant fighting only served to reveal how fearful and pow-erless they felt in their own lives. How absurd it seemed to fight over, violently defend, and devote your life to a doc-trine that could never be proven! And how fragile must your belief system be that you cannot entertain simple questions or engage in civil discussion about it? I resented their zealotry at the time, but as an adult, I am deeply appreciative of their desperation to convert me. Even as a juvenile, I could see how misguided it was to force a belief system on another sover-eign soul, so as a result of their dogmatic pursuits, I ultimately learned to trust my own intuition.

It was no surprise that my family leaned so heavily on their faith, as in my experience, those who have been disconnected from Source—and themselves—through trauma often find comfort in religion. The community of like minds can support nonthreatening social connections, and the rigidity of the belief and behavioral structures can provide the illusion of safety—and also a welcome distraction from the untreated pain that causes troubled souls to seek solace in controlled belief systems in the first place. If you are being told what to believe, it relieves you of the need to do your own critical thinking . . . but this does not, of course, erase the underlying trauma or prevent us from feeling it.

Both of my parents suffered significant trauma in their childhoods (as did their parents), and as far as I know, never got any help to address it. As a result, the stress and behavioral patterns they developed to deal with that trauma informed every decision they ever made and every interaction they ever had for the rest of their lives. This—combined with the fact that education and exposure to other ways of living were not prioritized in my family—resulted in them viewing the world fearfully, as a dangerous place to be approached with suspicion. By the time I graduated from college, both of them had lived their entire lives within roughly an hour's drive of where they were born, and had the myopic worldviews to prove it.

I grew up regularly hearing and experiencing (though never understanding) racism, sexism, misogyny, homophobia, and xenophobia from various family members. When the LA riots broke out in 1992, it was, according to my family, because "black people didn't have the sense or self-control to take care of their own neighborhoods." When the family living next door—whose daughter was my best friend—couldn't pay their bills one month, it was because "Mexicans don't have any work ethic." When I once shared my aspirations to travel the world and find ways to strengthen communities in developing countries, I was told to "find a nice man to cook and clean for, and just be happy I was taken care of." When one of my dearest friends came out as gay, my family ceased to call him by name, and instead dubbed him, "the gay caballero." When I decided to visit Egypt, I was called a "terrorist sympathizer" and asked how I could disrespect my country by "playing with a bunch of ragheads." Whenever a heavy or disabled person crossed the street too slowly for their taste, it was because "they [were] too lazy and stupid to take care of themselves." Whenever there was a car accident, it was because "those Asians can't see over the wheel and shouldn't be driving." The hatred was constant.

They weren't much kinder to me, telling me to "toughen up" in response to my sensitivity, advising that I "get over it" when I empathized with others in pain, and calling my visions "the work of the devil." They labeled my synesthesia "unnatural" and "against God's law" and told me that I needed to pray for forgiveness for whatever sin I must have committed to be born this way.

Eventually, I started to believe them and began making myself smaller, more "normal," in hopes of avoiding their judgment and criticism. Moreover, because I was so sensitive to other people's emotions, I began having trouble separating their emotions from my own. If I was angry, I couldn't tell whether the anger was really mine or my father's. If I felt sad, I couldn't tell whether the sadness was mine or my mother's. Before I knew it, I was stuck on a never-ending rollercoaster of emotions that probably didn't belong to me, but were making me miserable nonetheless.

My solution to this problem was becoming an expert people pleaser. I reasoned that by trying to make everyone happy—since I could so easily feel when they weren't—I would ultimately suffer less. So, I started subverting my own feelings and needs for those of the people around me, not realizing that each time I did that, I lost a little piece of myself.

It worked remarkably well, however, and I quickly learned that if I ignored my intuition, rejected every gut impulse I had, and kept my mouth shut, I ceased to be an interesting target, and they would leave me alone. I became quite adept at playing "normal" and did not realize that I was slowly sliding toward a complete loss of self. I began to suppress my gifts in earnest, believing that perhaps if I were more like them, they wouldn't torment me anymore and I would be safe. And just like that, my light began to go out.

# CHAPTER THREE

AT FIRST, I HAD no idea what assimilation to my family's way of being was costing me. All I knew was that I wanted the constant, abusive persecution to stop, so I made it my mission to overlook their hateful comments, cruel behavior, and frustratingly disconnected religious beliefs. I pasted a permanent smile on my face and became the quintessential good girl: I went to church with my family, got perfect grades, never caused any trouble, and pretended not to be miserable in our provincial little town. It seemed a small price to pay for peace . . . or so I thought.

What I had not counted on was the fact that however painful and destructive it was to live with the constant turmoil of being the family freak, it was not remotely comparable to the turmoil precipitated by the denial of one's soul. With every disavowal of my true feelings, I—like the proverbial dying man—slipped further and further away from the light.

As a child, I did not yet realize that everything you suppress comes back to torment you one way or another, sometimes like a subtle, insidious haunting, and sometimes like a screaming, vengeful banshee. While I have experienced both, my physical comeuppance for selling my soul came rather swiftly.

My emotional and spiritual misery began manifesting as physical illness, resulting in the onset of chronic and very severe migraines. By the time I was in grade school, my migraines had become completely debilitating. I was so constantly vomiting, in excruciating pain, exhausted for days at a time, and unable to tolerate light or sound that my baffled parents thought I had a brain tumor and started taking me to doctors.

Specialist after specialist insisted that nothing was wrong with me, but I knew better. Though modern medicine could not identify what was ailing me, I was buckling under the constant pressure to act like someone else, to force my spirit into a smaller, darker, more manageable box in order to avoid challenging or upsetting anyone.

From the outside, everything looked fine—great, even—but just beneath the surface lurked a bottomless, thirsty rage. I was in constant misery, and as my *joie de vivre* continued to fade, I became a magnet for dark people and dark experiences. Just as light attracts light, darkness attracts darkness.

There was a defining incident at my grandmother's house when I was very young, around five or six, when one of the other neighborhood families had brought their kids over to play. There was a little boy a few years older than me who seemed to have a peculiar fascination with me. His interest made me nervous, so I tried to avoid him, but when my parents were inside the house and the kids were all playing outside, he cornered me behind my grandmother's car, shoved me up against the garage door, and forced his fingers inside of me. I was paralyzed by shock, fear, and shame. Frozen, I didn't understand why he would do that to me, but because I was too terrified to punch or push him away, I also felt complicit, like I must have done something wrong, invited it, or deserved it somehow.

After he left me alone, my face burning with shame, I went into the house and told my mother what he had done. She said, "he's just being a silly boy," and told me not to make a big deal of it. Her minimization of his violation shattered me. The boy's intrusion had already made me feel worthless, powerless, and empty, but her reaction also left me feeling completely unprotected and alone (feelings that ultimately dominated my life, perspective, and behavior in relationships for many, many years, until I learned how to rid myself of those emotional imprints).

I did not realize at the time that her reaction was entirely informed by her own unresolved sexual trauma. I won't expand on that, as it is not my story to tell, but it is critical to understand that we inherit our stress patterns from the traumas of our parents, as they do from theirs, and they do from theirs, on and on forever until someone has the courage, the strength, and the wisdom to break those patterns of generational trauma.

When a child's boundaries are broken by early and inappropriate sexualization, their self-worth is shattered, and they lose the ability to truly know themselves, to feel safe in the world, and to relate freely with other humans. Childhood sexual abuse is also particularly treacherous in that the inherent destruction of a child's self-esteem makes them a target later in life. Energetically speaking, those wounds linger and speak to other predators, throwing open the door as if to say, "come on in, the water's warm." And like so many others, this is exactly what I experienced. This incident proved to be the first in a very long list of sexual assaults.

The attacks seemingly came from everywhere: would-be suitors, friends I thought I could trust, strangers in bars, a masseuse I "won" an hour with on a radio show, one of my college professors, three separate bosses, and countless coworkers. Some were as mild as unwanted fondling, while others were vicious rapes. But after a while, it mattered little, as the differences became more and more difficult for me to perceive, and slowly, all men became the enemy. I began seeing threats everywhere, regarding all men as dangerous predators—and to me, they very often were, because that was the reality I had experienced up to that point. However, I had no idea that I had created—and was actively contributing to—that reality.

I realize that, for most people, the idea that anyone could possibly bear any responsibility for the horrible actions perpetrated against them by another is a radical—even offensive—thought. When this truth was first put to me by a dear friend and incredibly gifted healer, I had the same response; I was utterly enraged at the mere suggestion that I should be held accountable for any of the things done *to* me. What I did not know at the time is that we create our own experience of life, drawing experiences to us that teach us the lessons our soul wants to learn—and thus are responsible for the things that "happen" to us.

But this realization—and the revolutionary healing it offers—only became available to me after an intense and grueling journey of spiritual awakening, which set me on the path to remembering the true nature of my soul underneath all of the negative programming I had experienced and recovering my true self. While I spent years seeking various forms of healing, including counseling, travel, education, and self-help programs like Landmark and Avatar (all of which taught me something useful, but in retrospect, I view them as preschool compared with the graduate education that was coming), that journey truly began the moment I met my husband.

# CHAPTER FOUR

It was August 2004 and I had just ended a very serious relationship that was headed for marriage. I had entered into this relationship very young, prior to doing the work necessary to resolve my trauma, so it was the damaged version of myself—seeking healing—who chose that partnership. I (unconsciously) sought out the furthest possible thing from the men I had been surrounded by as a child: someone kind, gentle, well-mannered, respectful, and, most importantly, safe.

I truly thought I loved him. After all, in addition to being a man who would never hurt me, he was handsome, educated, affable, and well liked by most everyone in my life. Having nothing to compare the experience to, I figured it must be love. But as I began to seek help dealing with my past, explore the limiting beliefs my experience had created, and grow to new levels of understanding and functionality, I found myself increasingly uninterested in the relationship, and I began to crave the intellectual and physical stimulation I didn't know I desperately needed.

It took me a few years to realize that what I felt for him was a familial love, the great fondness one might have for a dear friend, coupled with gratitude for the lessons he taught me. It was not a romantic love. Moreover, even after years together, I still did not trust him. But this is far more a commentary on my traumatic past and state of development than his character, as he had never done anything to earn my distrust.

In retrospect, I realize that he was in my life to teach me that there were men in the world who would not abuse me, assault me, or take advantage of me—and I will always be grateful to him for being such a good and decent man that he was able to teach me that lesson. But in my inexperience at the time, I took my feelings, or lack thereof, to mean that I was incapable of truly loving or trusting a man, decided that I must not be cut out for long-term relationships, and left him. I resolved never to get married or have children, as I didn't want to be responsible for bringing children into a miserable world to be raised by miserable people in a miserable marriage, as that had certainly been my experience.

To celebrate my escape from monogamy, I took a trip to the Virgin Islands with two of my girlfriends. After a glorious week of carefree adventures and sun-soaked freedom, beholden to absolutely no one, I became even more certain that I was meant to be alone, free from the constraints of a relationship. I didn't want a partner, as I had only ever felt suppressed and exhausted by a man. I couldn't imagine a relationship that actually excited or invigorated me.

Reluctant to leave St. Thomas and return to San Diego (where I was taking some time off between college and grad school), my friends and I had stayed on the beach until the last possible minute before heading to the airport. More concerned with squeezing out every last bit of the experience than looking chic, we boarded the plane in our bikinis and sweats, sandy, sunburned, and happily sleepy. I relaxed into my aisle seat with a blanket and a novel, intending to ignore everyone for the next several hours.

The plane took off as scheduled, and we made the quick hop to San Juan to pick up several more passengers before continuing on to NYC (where we intended to make a short stop before heading back to California). I was fully engrossed in my novel, paying little attention to the passengers trickling on board, when suddenly, the most beautiful man I had ever seen in my life stepped onto the plane.

I have never been easily entranced by physical beauty, valuing virtues like brilliance, confidence, and courage much more. However, I couldn't take my eyes off this man. It was more than his towering height, muscular body, radiant skin, and perfectly sculpted jawline. His aura was luminous. Though I had shut down my gifts years earlier and had largely ignored their persistent rumblings ever since, I couldn't help but see that his energy was undeniably divine, swirling in radiant, golden convolutions all around him. He was angelic and graceful, and I had never felt anything like him.

"God help me, this is the last thing I need," I thought, and immediately slumped down in the cramped airplane seat and hid behind my book. As he walked down the aisle on my side of the jumbo jet, I held my breath until he passed me. But just when I thought I was safe, he took the center aisle seat slightly behind and next to mine.

Willing myself to look straight ahead, I read the same sentence of my book over and over again, not comprehending a word, barely able to focus with his energy so close to me. And just then, I heard a voice behind me say, "Excuse me?" I turned around to see him smiling at me. "Does your phone have a stock ticker on it?" It didn't, and I didn't even know what that was at the time, but nonetheless, we started chatting, and quickly fell deep into conversation. I learned that his name was Joe and I was delighted to discover that my instincts were right on, as he was as intelligent, kind, and interesting as he was handsome, and the hours together flew by.

Now, I failed to mention that earlier, when we left St. Thomas, a tropical storm was brewing, and it had followed us to San Juan, picking up steam as it traveled. Joe and I were so deep in conversation during the flight from San Juan to New York that we didn't notice the flight taking longer than usual until the captain announced that we would have to reroute from JFK to Newark because that tropical storm had turned into the now-infamous Hurricane Charley and was traveling up the coast wreaking havoc. So we headed for Newark . . . but so did countless other flights, and we ended up circling the runway for hours until we finally ran out of gas and had to make an emergency landing.

Even after finally landing, our plane was stuck way out on the tarmac, terribly far from the airport. It was miserably hot inside the stuffy cabin, we had long since run out of food and water, and an older gentleman on the plane wasn't doing very well. He seemed to be suffering from dehydration and disorientation and ultimately had a cardiac episode on the plane! Joe, who I later learned was in medical school, jumped to his aid and helped save his life right in front of me.

As emergency vehicles made their way out to our remote location, the storm caught up to us. It started pouring rain and lightning began to strike the tarmac. The captain finally released us from the plane, and we sprinted toward the shelter of the airport. Inside, it was melee, with hundreds of displaced passengers frantically trying to figure out how to get where they were going. As lightning continued to strike dangerously close to the airport, a voice over the loudspeaker announced that all outgoing flights were canceled for the duration of the storm. With nowhere to go and no way out of the airport, people panicked, became angry, and a riot quickly ensued. Joe and I were separated in the hysteria, and despite my stubborn insistence that I was not interested in a relationship, my heart sank when I realized that I had not given him my contact information and would probably never see him again.

Just as I was beginning to regret my obstinance and wonder if perhaps the universe was trying to tell me something, I saw Joe, pushing his way back to me through the crowd. To my delight, he asked for my phone number.

He got out on a flight that night, but my friends and I were stuck in the airport for nearly two days before we managed to get a flight—with three connections—back to San Diego. Upon my return home, Joe started calling me. Initially, I did not pick up the phone, as I had convinced myself that he was too perfect and lived too far away, and that nothing could possibly come of it. Every time I saw his name pop up on my phone, I felt a deep longing and tinge of regret, but stubbornly refused to talk to him.

This continued for weeks until, finally, I was unable to resist anymore. When I picked up the phone, nearly paralyzed with fear and anticipation, the warmth of his voice washed over me, and I felt as if I was right back on that plane with him. I apologized for not picking up the phone for so long, and he told me that he had been about to give up on me, and that this was the last time he had intended to call. I silently thanked God for making me pick up that phone!

After that, Joe and I started talking almost every day. What started off as one- or two-hour conversations quickly turned into nightly four-, five-, and six-hour conversations. Because of the time difference and the fact that we both had roommates, I would hide in my closet and talk to him, while he would hang out on his porch or in his kitchen all night. We would often talk until the sun came up. I think our longest conversation exceeded nine hours.

This continued for over a year. Though we never saw each other (and this was before the days of FaceTime), we spoke nearly every day. Though we spent more time talking to each other than anyone else in our lives—including the people we were dating—neither of us realized that we were falling in love. Finally, we decided to see each other in person again, and I made the trip out to Boston. The rest, as they say, is history. We immediately realized we were madly in love with each other and couldn't stand to be apart. I had all of my belongings packed and shipped from California, and we moved in together. We were engaged within six months and got married in 2008 . . . back in the Virgin Islands, where it all began.

# CHAPTER FIVE

OUR DAYS TOGETHER WERE blissful. Being together was euphoric beyond anything I had ever experienced. Between our intense connection, our riveting conversations, and our inexhaustible passion, we quite literally couldn't get enough of each other. We were perfect partners, beautifully in sync in every way.

Though I had been so certain that I wasn't the relationship type, had always needed plenty of time alone, and deeply valued my space, I had never been so happy as I was with my Joe, crammed into the first home we ever purchased together—an itty bitty 560-square-foot condo in Cambridge. Though we lived right on top of each other in that snug little space, we loved it. If we weren't snuggled up on our loveseat talking or side by side working on our laptops in silent companionship, we were laughing gregariously while cooking in our tiny galley kitchen. I had never imagined this kind of love was even possible, much less that I would ever be so blessed as to experience it. But despite our passionate, endless love for each other, we could not outrun our pasts, and slowly, our lingering traumas began to creep into our relationship.

I noticed when I met Joe that he had a tendency to emotionally withdraw, especially as we got closer, and that very often, he was simply not present. Though my husband was as sweet, kind, and thoughtful as the day I met him, there was also a persistent, haunting darkness that, though it didn't belong to him, clung to him like cigarette smoke on cashmere. It was always present, overshadowing our loving connection. Anytime we argued or encountered a stressful situation, the strangest thing happened: his radiant, larger-than-life force would start to diminish, as if someone was choking off the flow of energy to his soul, until his light went completely dark and he vanished right in front of my eyes. His physical body was there, sitting next to me, but there was nobody home. He became robotic, icy, dispassionate, and unresponsive. Nothing about this chilling stranger resembled the man I had fallen in love with, and it was unnerving.

He eventually confided in me that in his childhood, he had experienced horrific sexual abuse at the hands of a family friend. Like many children whose boundaries are broken so young that they are unable to process what happened, he forced it out of his mind and told himself that it was behind him, and thus no longer affected him. Of course, that is unfortunately not how the human psyche works, and the closer he and I became, the more he was triggered by our intimacy.

It didn't matter how close we were or how much trust existed between us; any stressor at all, large or small, would immediately pull him out of his body, and I would watch him disappear right in front of me. His eyes went blank, his posture changed, his expression became vacant, his affect became flat, and I could feel his heart close, as if he had encased it in armor. Mere moments after being as close as two people could possibly be, he would become unreachable, and I would become the enemy. He stayed this way for hours, days, and sometimes weeks at a time. Then, without warning, the real Joe would suddenly resurface and have no awareness of ever having been gone. It was excruciating, lonely, and heartbreaking—especially since I knew it wasn't his fault or something he could help. I could clearly see his beautiful soul, even when he was in the depths of his disappearing act, and I was desperate to free him, but didn't know where to begin. The longer we were together, the farther out of reach he seemed to get, and our happy relationship began to crumble.

This was further complicated by the fact that I was also suffering. Finding my true partner in Joe had taught me what unconditional love—which I had never experienced in my birth family—really is, and being loved so purely had finally given me the freedom to be my true self, rather than the small, non-threatening version of myself that I pretended to be as a child in order to be accepted. As a result, returning home to visit my family of origin had become a very unpleasant and confusing experience for me; it knocked me off center and began to unearth deep resentment and unbridled rage that I did not realize was simmering just below my sanguine exterior.

My parents were both deeply unhappy people in an obviously abusive and joyless marriage. My father was an enigma. To the outside world, he was endlessly charming, charismatic, and gracious. But at home with my sister, my mother, and me, he was an extremely controlling, hostile man with a hair-trigger temper and constant mood swings. He was cruel, unpredictable, and seemed to enjoy destroying the self-esteem and self-worth of others, especially those who depended on him. A master salesman—and a master of gaslighting—he could convince just about anyone of just about anything, and he used those talents to convince everyone in our lives that he was a kind, wonderful, caring husband and father.

Though almost obsessive about being perceived as a perfect, successful family man, he was deeply antisocial, narcissistic, and lived in his own reality with very clear and rigid ideas about how the world—and everyone in it—should function. When anyone or anything failed to live up to his expectations, however fantastical, he would become enraged and often violent. He did not physically abuse us, but he frequently threw things, punched holes in walls, kicked things, broke things, and otherwise destroyed property. We used to have pictures hanging in odd places all over our house and garage to cover the holes he had put through our walls in fits of rage. He was emotionally unstable, generously praising us one moment and viciously berating us the next.

There was no room for any of us to be ourselves around him; he expected perfection and strict obedience to his rule, and anything less guaranteed that you would be severely punished. I remember when we would hear his car pull into the driveway every afternoon after work, and my mother would frantically run through the house turning off the music, straightening up anything that was out of place, pulling the curtains shut, and banishing us to our rooms. She was always trying to curate the circumstances of his arrival, desperate to minimize the chances that he would explode the moment he walked through the door. I was absolutely terrified of him, as his personality would change in an instant, and so I never knew what to expect from him. My mother used to call him Dr. Jekyll and Mr. Hyde. As a result of his unpredictability, I learned never to count on him, and—ultimately—not to trust men (which can prove problematic in a young marriage).

Now, of course, as an adult, I can clearly see that these behaviors were the result of his intense fears of abandonment, instability, and not being loved or valued, likely stemming from his own childhood. And despite all the misery we lived through, I do have some wonderful memories of my father, like the time I was three or four years old and he sat me in his lap and taught me the words to "Surfer Girl," which we would sing together for years afterward, and the rare occasions when he was in the mood to talk instead of fight, and we would chat for hours about everything under the sun. But these occasions were few and far between, and as a particularly gentle, hyper-sensitive little girl trying to find love and security in the world, he terrified and confused me, and I never felt safe around him.

In contrast, my mother was warmer and more loving, but also passive, powerless, and insecure—the perpetual victim. She never got the help she needed after enduring chronic sexual abuse in her childhood, so she grew up with very low self-esteem, understandably fearful of the world, and unsur-prisingly married a controlling man with a desperate need for power and dominance.

Between my mother's history of abuse and the fact that she moved straight from her parents' house to my father's house, she never had a chance to explore and grow into herself, and thus never developed much of an identity. Emotionally and economically dependent on my father, she threw herself into becoming the seemingly perfect wife and mother and became an expert in the arts of pacification and denial.

My parents fought constantly. I have countless memories of lying awake in my bed at night, listening to my father tear-ing into my mother while she cried. He seemed to take par-ticular pleasure in starting fights in the car right before we arrived at a family or public function, so that he would exit the car polished and smiling, while the three of us would be distraught and sobbing. The only thing worse than my father screaming at my mother (or us) was his version of the silent treatment, when he would quietly quake with rage, trembling and gurgling like a venting volcano, leaving us to guess when he would finally erupt. My mother dealt with this by developing a rich fantasy life and becoming an adept people pleaser (sound familiar?), constantly submitting to his unreasonable demands and explosive temper.

Though she always pretended to be happy—throwing herself into Tupperware parties, Girl Scout troops, and the PTA—she deeply resented motherhood. Though she loved us in her way, she also hated us for anchoring her to my father. It was very clear to me from an early age that my mother had found herself living a life she hadn't planned on and didn't want. She wanted her freedom, and my sister and I were the only things standing in the way. She told me on multiple occasions that she had considered suicide, specifically by running her car into a brick wall, but chose to stay alive for us. She always said this with the clear implication that we should feel loved and valued by her choice to keep sticking it out for us, but it was obvious that she blamed us for trapping her there. Unlike many children of divorce, I constantly wished that my parents would split up and end our misery.

When I was fifteen, my mother had finally had enough. She moved out and left my sister and me with my father and moved to a new city to start a new life. She got her own apartment, went back to school, and started dating, and though I was proud of her for standing up for herself at last, I was also furious with her for not protecting herself or her children for all those years. Disappointed and disgusted, I felt like she had failed us, and it took me a long time to forgive her for what I perceived as her weakness. I also resented her for leaving us behind for my father to continue abusing. In retrospect, I know she wasn't capable of setting a better example, but at the time, I was deeply hurt by her actions. She eventually moved back to town, remarried (a young, irresponsible man-child, opposite of my father in every way), and tried to reestablish our family, but the damage was already done.

Having already taken many measures to deal with my trauma before I met my husband, I truly (and foolishly) thought I had moved past it. Since Joe and I lived 3,000 miles away from my family and thus rarely saw them, I no longer spent time thinking about my unhappy childhood and was becoming happier and more myself every day. But upon returning to the site of my tumultuous upbringing after experiencing true love and acceptance with Joe, the differences were glaring and deeply disturbing for me.

I remember the first time I brought Joe home with me to a family gathering. I could tell he was not enjoying himself, but I chalked it up to nerves and the fact that my family was difficult to be around. However, I later found out that the real problem was me! He told me that I turned into a completely different person around my family. At first, I was defensive and disbelieving, but after taking an honest look at the situation, I realized that he was right; when I was around my family, I slipped right back into the small, superficial, unobjectionable, safety-mode version of myself that I had created when trying to survive them years earlier. I decided that I never wanted to change myself for another person again, and I recognized that I clearly had more work to do.

After that, it became increasingly difficult to be around them. With each reluctant trip home—as I still called it at the time—their self-delusion, jealousy, and hatefulness became harder and harder to withstand. They were so unhappy that our happiness only seemed to make them angrier and more resentful. Thanks to Joe calling out my coping mechanism and the damage it was doing to both of us, I could no longer pretend that I didn't see their behavior clearly, or that it didn't bother me. Their dysfunctional, combative style of interaction stood in such brutal juxtaposition to our loving relationship that being in their presence became very stressful and started to make me physically ill. Whenever I was around them, my migraines became absolutely unbearable and my nausea and stomach pain got so bad that I couldn't keep anything down. Their dark energy was literally making me sick, and the illness always lingered long after I left them. After a handful of lengthy, back-to-back visits, the cumulative stress became too much, and I eventually stopped eating altogether and became very underweight. My health steadily began to deteriorate until I found myself in a state of chronic illness and pain—which put even more stress on my already-struggling marriage.

# CHAPTER SIX

THOUGH JOE AND I were going through an intensely difficult period, my personal reawakening was just beginning. Since meeting Joe and finally experiencing the freedom to be myself, my long-suppressed intuitive gifts had begun to stir.

As a child, I constantly saw the numbers 416 everywhere: on clocks, on license plates, on billboards, on mailboxes, on paperwork, etc. It seemed that everywhere I looked, there they were. At the time, I didn't think this was unusual, because 4/16 is my birth date, so I assumed, in my childish logic, that everyone saw their birth date numbers everywhere. I had never thought much of it, but after meeting Joe, I started seeing more numerical patterns. I regularly saw 1111, 222, 333, and 555 *everywhere*. For a period of nearly two years, I woke up at 3:33 am every single night, without fail. I wondered, of course, whether my brain was playing tricks on me or whether there could be some other logical explanation for this phenomenon, as I never consciously sought out any of these numerical patterns. However, I continued to see them several times every day. Though I didn't know what to make of it, it certainly felt like someone or something was trying to get my attention.

At the same time, my visions had returned and were increasing in both frequency and accuracy. I began to have daily visions about little things, like who I would run into at the grocery store or what old friend would happen to call me that afternoon. They came like clockwork and always proved true, and in retrospect, I believe these visions were designed to convince me that my gift was to be taken seriously and to prepare me for what was coming.

In 2010, I had the opportunity to go to Egypt with my graduate school professor and some of my classmates. I was elated, as I had always been strongly called to visit Egypt, and of course, had been seeing it in dreams and visions since I was a child. Joe was in the middle of his medical residency at the time and could not join me, so I packed my bags and set off, eager to discover what awaited me there.

I found Egypt extraordinary in every conceivable way. The country was beyond beautiful, with an arid climate and majestic desert landscape unlike anything I had ever seen. The sight of families fishing and bathing along the fertile banks of the Nile in contrast with the stunning backdrop of massive, ancient ruins and endless sand dunes behind them was startling and magical. The people were warm, kind, and very welcoming. The women in particular made a constant effort to seek me out, ensure that I was happy and comfortable, and include me in their conversations and experiences. The food was remarkably fresh, flavorful, and delicious, full of intoxicating, aromatic spices and devoid of the chemicals and preservatives to which we are so accustomed in the US. The communities were modest and lovely, teeming with playful children running through the streets, open-air markets bursting with dried fruit, scarves, and spices, and ornate, beautiful mosques on seemingly every corner. Walking through the streets of Egypt was like going back in time, and I found the sheer age and history of this ancient land, replete with temples and monuments erected in celebration thousands of years before North America was even settled, a deeply humbling experience.

Though I was a tourist in a land 5,000 miles from my home, I felt oddly comfortable—and oddly healthy—from the moment I arrived; my migraines curiously disappeared, I started sleeping again, and my appetite returned. We landed in Cairo and spent a few days exploring the magnificence of the city before making our way down to the Temple of Karnak in the ancient city of Thebes, known in modernity as Luxor. Karnak is a massive, sprawling complex, having been developed over more than 1,000 years by roughly thirty pharaohs. Considered the largest religious site in the world, it is a dizzying labyrinth of temples, chapels, obelisks, pylons, and pillars. As I wandered into the Precinct of Amon-Re, awestruck, I began to feel a familiar swirling, tingly heat in my feet and legs that slowly migrated up into my chest, where it began to pound. With every step I took, I could feel the pulsating energy coming up from the ground and emanating from the ruins surrounding me . . . it was all so familiar.

I walked into the Great Hypostyle Hall, which boasts 134 enormous sandstone columns in the shape of papyrus stalks, each richly decorated with inscriptions from Sety I, Ramesses II, and their successors. Mesmerized, I felt drawn toward one particular column. When I placed my hand on it, I was immediately gripped by what felt like an electric current fusing my hand to the column, shooting down my arm and into my body. It paralyzed me, and I stood there, rooted in place. My eyes closed involuntarily, and that electricity shot into my arm and fused with the pulsating energy in my chest. Behind my closed lids, I saw the very same view of the temple I had been enjoying seconds earlier—but thousands of years ago. I was looking through my own eyes down the long corridor of giant columns, but instead of being silent, deserted, and in ruins, they were overflowing with people and humming with activity. I saw thousands of people packed into the temple, some in robes and linens, some in soldier's regalia, many with instruments, all excited and celebratory . . . and all looking in my direction. Rows of priests, carrying large platforms with golden sculptures atop them, were moving in a long processional, and I was being led onto an elevated platform and seated in an ornate, golden chair of sorts. To my right, I felt a powerful masculine presence seated next to me. Though I could not see him, I could feel that we were deeply connected and knew he was important to me. While looking out over the great festival taking place at my feet, my nose filled with the heady scents of freshly baked bread and roasted game.

I felt a hand on my shoulder and my eyes snapped open, energy shooting violently out of my crown. One of my travel companions was jostling my arm with concern, wanting to know whether I was OK, and as quickly as the vision had come on, it disappeared. Stunned at what I had just seen and quite dizzy from the experience, I sat down for a moment. I realized in disbelief that I had just seen a much fuller, more elaborate version of the very same vision I had been having since I was a little girl—at the actual site where it took place. I felt like I had just discovered a missing piece of my own history, but struggled with disbelief. Could that really have just happened?

I continued to mull over my trip back in time as we traveled south to visit the Valley of Nobles and Medinet Habu, the mortuary temple of Ramesses III. We then sailed down the Nile for four days, visiting Esna, the Temple of Horus at Edfu, and the unique double temple of Kom Ombo, dedicated to both Sobek and Horus. I gleefully soaked up every fascinating site, tour, and bit of history I could, but I did not experience anything resembling what happened at Karnak, and I could not put it out of my mind.

Finally, we arrived in the breathtakingly beautiful Nubian city of Aswan, where we visited the ancient Philae Temple of Isis. As I walked the grounds, I noticed that I felt nothing from the ground beneath the temple, but every time I touched the temple walls, a little shock of electricity would zing right through me. Finally, I came to an open-air structure made of columns that was situated on a hill directly overlooking the Nile. As I walked between two of the columns and leaned out over the water, a huge gust of wind blew through them and nearly knocked me off my feet. I reached my hands out and grabbed the columns for balance, and it happened again: I felt that magical, dancing energy surge up through my body, radiate up into my head, fuse my hands to the columns, and force my eyes shut. There, hovering right in front of me, Isis herself appeared, tiny at first, her golden-winged body growing larger and larger until she dwarfed me. When she wrapped her great wings around me, I felt indescribable euphoria and peace, as if she had filled my body with pure, radiant, heavenly light and driven out every bit of human doubt, anxiety, and fear. I stood there, bathing in her radiance, until I felt myself coming back to the present moment.

As I opened my eyes, I wondered why I had felt nothing remarkable from the grounds themselves, but radiant, divine energy from the actual temple ruins. While chatting with our group's assigned Egyptologist later that evening, I discovered that the construction of the Aswan High Dam in 1960 had flooded the temple's original site and put it at risk of total submersion, so it was deconstructed, moved, and rebuilt on its current site. Unable to deny what I had experienced, I pondered what the universe was trying to communicate as we made our way back to the hotel.

The next morning, we flew out to the western bank of Lake Nasser to visit the magnificent twin temples of Abu Simbel. Originally cut into living rock by Ramesses II (like Philae, Abu Simbel was moved in the 1960s to escape flood damage due to the Aswan High Dam), the massive Great Temple stands nearly 100 feet tall, and is the most awe-inspiring structure I have ever seen. I was hypnotized by its size, precision of construction, and startling level of preservation, and soon wandered away from my group to explore on my own. As I passed through the main hall in the Great Temple and made my way to the farthest of the outer side chambers, I found myself alone in a long, dark, narrow hallway. At the very end of the dimly lit corridor, I thought I saw a section of hieroglyphics faintly glowing. Disbelieving, I blinked, thinking it was perhaps a trick of the eye, but the glow remained. I followed the shadowy light all the way to the dead end, and the closer I got to the light, the heavier and thicker the air felt, almost like I was wading through thick, dense fog. I reached the end of the chamber and the glow promptly disappeared, but I instinctively reached out to touch the place that had been lit moments earlier.

The moment my hand met the stone, electricity surged through my body and—just as it had at Karnak—fused my hand to the wall. A montage of scenes started racing through my mind, one rapid-fire image chasing the next. They moved so quickly that I could hardly absorb one before it disappeared into the next. They were images of Hathor, goddess of love, beauty, pleasure, and fertility, using her mastery of vibration in myriad ways, including to heal wounded bodies and souls, to help women through arduous childbirths, to ward off attackers with harmful intent, to experience divine sexual pleasure, and to bring souls together in loving connection. Though every vignette featured Hathor, each scene was deeply familiar, and I could feel my own presence in the periphery, like I had either been physically present for these events or somehow otherwise experienced her powerful vibrations. It was as if she was prodding me to remember, reminding me that I hold the magnificent power of the divine feminine, which has been so long suppressed on this plane, and asking me to awaken and use my vibration to anchor it on earth once again.

The whole reel flew by in what seemed like moments. From deep in my reverie, I heard someone calling my name. It took me a second to realize that the voice was real, not part of the vision, and I suddenly snapped out of it. It was one of my fellow grad students, with whom I was traveling. She told me the group had been looking for me for nearly an hour, and that it was time to leave. I was stunned, as my experience had seemed to last only seconds.

As we made our way back to the airport, I ruminated on what I had seen, why it had been shown to me, and what—in combination with my experiences at Karnak and Philae—it all meant for me.

The next morning, we flew back up to Cairo and made our way to Giza to visit the pyramids. Unlike so many bucket list attractions that turned out to be a bit disappointing (looking at you, *Mona Lisa*), the Great Pyramid is an absolute engineering marvel, and much larger and more impressive than I ever imagined. Originally built at a height of 481 feet, it still stands 454 feet tall after roughly 4,500 years. Each of the stones that look like tiny bricks on film are actually 1 meter long, 2.5 meters wide, and 1–1.5 meters high, and weigh 6.5–10 tons each! It is difficult to comprehend just how massive this structure really is until you are standing humbly beneath it, struggling to see the top.

Very eager to get inside, I was relieved to snag the last entrance ticket issued that day. I climbed up the steep, rocky exterior of the Great Pyramid to Robber's Tunnel, an alternate and much-storied entrance to the tomb. (According to many historians, Muslim ruler Caliph Al-Ma'mun purportedly created the passage in order to remove stolen treasure from the tomb, while others believe the passage was created centuries before the Muslims even came to Egypt.) I made my way inside.

I soon learned that the climb up to Khufu's tomb is not for the faint of heart. As I stepped inside the pyramid, a stifling combination of intense heat, oppressive humidity, and the scent of ammonia hit me in nauseating waves. The confining walls of the Ascending Passage suddenly felt more like a cramped hothouse than a sacred burial chamber and I silently thanked my professor for bringing us in March instead of July. I made my way past the Queen's Chamber and finally came to the Grand Gallery—the 69-foot final climb up to the King's Chamber. There are no stairs; instead, you must pull yourself up a slick ramp—with only raised crossties for traction—at a very steep incline. The passage is incredibly narrow, 6.9 feet wide at its widest point and only 3.4 feet wide at its narrowest, and the ceiling is very low, so you must stoop down and bend over while you are climbing in order to make it through. To further complicate matters, tourists are packed into the tunnel like Vienna sausages and the way up is also the way down, so while you are pulling yourself precariously up the sweaty, slippery passage, others are simultaneously negotiating their way back down (and in many cases, grabbing errant arms or legs or whatever is available for leverage when they slip; imagine a live version of Chutes and Ladders gone horribly awry). Not having known any of this before my arrival, I was woefully ill-dressed and had chosen most unfortunate footwear for the occasion—flip-flops. Needless to say, it was not an easy trip up and I have only the grace of God and the reliable grip of my well-trained dancer's toes to thank for my survival.

I finally completed the treacherous ascent and made it up into the King's Chamber, a roughly 34 x 17-foot empty room made entirely of pink granite, where only Khufu's empty sarcophagus remains. There were several other travelers milling around the room, but I immediately noticed a group of Tibetan monks gathering near the sarcophagus. I watched, curious, as they encircled it and began to join hands. To my great surprise, two of the monks crossed the room toward me, each took one of my hands, and they pulled me into their circle. I couldn't imagine why they had singled me out, but I was honored and utterly fascinated. They closed their eyes and began to chant, their powerful, melodic voices quickly entrancing me. As the monks' voices grew louder and deeper, the chatter of tourists and damp, dank smells of the tomb fell away, until I lost all sense of where I was. I began to feel that familiar warmth tingling in my gut. As their voices, primal and beautiful, grew louder still, I felt heat coming from each of the unfamiliar hands holding mine. My hands and arms began to vibrate with intense, pulsating energy that shot out through my fingers, intermingling with the energy coming from my companions, and though we were encased in cement with no windows or door to the outside, a powerful, swirling wind suddenly arose and began to whip my hair across my face. The energy raced around and around our circle, flowing from each one of us to the next, until it was moving so fast that I could no longer differentiate mine from theirs and it became one continuous, pulsating stream. The stream abruptly burst forth, expanding into the center of our circle and filling it with a column of light that shot directly up through the apex of the pyramid and into the heavens. It felt like a portal was opening, as if we were standing at the ends of the earth, at the gateway of the divine. Paralyzed in a blissful state of cosmic oneness with these beautiful strangers, I have no idea how much time passed. Finally, I felt the energy begin to weaken and the light column fade away, and we released our hands. The two gentlemen who had pulled me into the circle bowed to me, and I to them, in a silent display of mutual respect and recognition of the divine miracle we had just witnessed.

As I turned away from the circle, I noticed that only two of the other tourists in the room seemed to have noticed our extraordinary experience, as they stood there with their mouths agape, plastered against the walls of the tomb, clearly trying to make sense of what they had just witnessed. One of them looked incredulous, but delighted, while the other looked utterly terrified. Everyone else was simply wandering around, chatting and pointing out interesting aspects of the sarcophagus, as if they hadn't seen a thing. At the time, I couldn't explain why some saw the column of light and some didn't any more than I could explain why the monks pulled me into their circle.

As I made my way shakily back down the Grand Gallery passage, lightheaded and a bit dizzy, I marveled at what had just occurred. As unexpected and surprising as that—and every other experience I had here—was, the strangest part was that it really didn't feel strange at all. I realized that somehow, I felt more genuinely at home here, in this land of mysticism and magic, than I had ever felt anywhere else on earth. I was also confounded by how much better my health was here. I hadn't felt that good in several years!

Later, as I boarded the long flight home and bid Egypt farewell, I knew that something had permanently shifted inside of me. After years of suppressing my abilities, downplaying—or outright disregarding—clear signs and synchronicities, and ignoring the persistent rumblings of my gut, my experiences here had shaken something loose, and I couldn't deny who I was anymore. It felt like a light had come on in a dark attic, and though I had no idea what was coming, I knew that I had just experienced a spiritual rite of passage that would alter the course of my life forever.

# CHAPTER SEVEN

UPON RETURNING FROM MY remarkable trip, I was on quite a spiritual high and ruthlessly optimistic about my future as well as the future of my relationship with Joe. My life-changing experiences in Egypt had opened my eyes and I had begun to realize how much more was possible than my familial and religious limitations had ever allowed me to conceive. Everything felt beautiful, magical, exciting, and new, and I truly believed that I had been released from the wounds of my childhood. I couldn't wait to charge into the future with my newfound idealism, vowing to simply leave the past behind me and start fresh.

But that is, of course, not how the human psyche works. Trauma doesn't simply disappear because you decide that it should, or because you have a wonderful experience that temporarily takes its place at the forefront of your mind. It remains there, dormant, fiendishly manipulating your perspective and waiting to be triggered again.

I did not realize at the time that with each new level of awakening comes a more discriminating awareness of the areas in which you are still asleep, controlled by false narratives created in response to past wounds. The light has a way of putting the darkness into rather harsh contrast and making abundantly clear what is not working in your life, as I would soon discover.

Shortly after my return from Egypt, Joe and I decided to start a family. I had to stop taking my migraine medication—which I had been on for many years at this point—in order to get pregnant safely, and my health started deteriorating very rapidly. My migraines became unbearable and I was in constant agony. I soon became pregnant, and though, mercifully, our sweet baby boy remained safe and healthy, I had a terrible time and was in and out of the hospital for weeks at a time throughout my entire pregnancy. In addition to the chronic migraines, I had severe hyperemesis gravidarum, vomited dozens of times a day, frequently lost consciousness, and couldn't even keep down enough water to stay hydrated. I ultimately had to be put on an IV to get adequate fluids.

Very early in my pregnancy, I made the mistake of going home to see my birth family. First of all, I shouldn't have been traveling, as sick as I was (my doctors had already put me on medication to control the excessive vomiting and the pain), and second of all, I should have known that being around them was only going to make matters worse. The visit ended up being the last time I ever referred to that place as "home."

In truth, my family behaved the same way they had always behaved; it was I who had changed. With my eyes open wider than ever before—and a precious life growing in my belly—I could no longer tolerate their toxicity, jealously, resentment, and hatefulness. In my severely weakened state, I was unable to ignore it or block it out, and I quickly found their presence unbearable. I was wracked with guilt for not wanting to be around the people who raised me, and my refusal to deal with the true source of my misery only deepened my suffering.

To make matters worse, my mother seemed to take great pleasure in my pain and took every available opportunity to exacerbate it. She had told me on many occasions over the years that she wished her life had been different: that she hadn't married my father, that she had stayed with her child-hood boyfriend, that she had gone away to college, that she had lived on the east coast, that she had seen the world before having children . . . her list of regrets was long. So, when I took off the moment I graduated from high school, desperate to get out of the small town I grew up in and experience the world on my own terms, she was very unhappy with me. It was clear that she resented my life experience, my education, my travels, and certainly my happy marriage.

My early childhood experience had taught me not to trust my family, to only count on myself, and to never show them any weakness. This was the first time I had truly been vulnerable around them and she relished every second of it. The fact that I was struggling and in pain seemed to invigorate her and she was deliberately cold and callous, exploiting every weakness I had. I now know that what she really hated was the weakness in herself, but at the time, I was devastated by her cruelty, and I knew I had to get out. I was far too weak and sick to travel alone, but I could not be in their presence a moment longer, so I left that day, went to a cheap motel near the airport, and waited three days until my wonderful husband—always my hero—was able to leave his residency and fly out to get me.

The months that followed brought me incredible sadness, but also incredible growth. Breaking away from my family was very difficult and very painful, but my husband and son gave me the strength to finally draw the boundaries I sorely needed. At first, I had intended the split to be temporary; I knew I wasn't seeing clearly and had to step away from all of them to get some perspective and figure out what I really wanted. I went through a long mourning period, but every time I felt the urge to reach out, I asked myself whether I actually wanted to speak to them, or whether I was just uncomfortable with the sudden absence of everything I was used to. It was always the latter, and as the months went on, I realized that not only was I doing the right thing for myself and my chosen family, but that I did not miss my birth family. In truth, my life was far more joyful and peaceful without them.

Instead of making any effort to repair the situation, they did their best to punish me from afar by starting myriad rumors, and they encouraged family friends and relatives to cut me out of their lives. For the most part, the people who believed the rumors and acquiesced to the pressure to disown me were those I wasn't close to and who didn't know me very well, so they weren't terribly meaningful losses. Thanks to the education of my childhood, I already knew how easy it was to manipulate fundamentalists (in this case, the religious variety) into senseless action by convincing them that someone has irretrievably strayed from the flock and thus poses an existential threat to their well-being.

However, there were a few losses that truly shocked me, as they were of people I had been very close to since childhood (or so I believed) and had trusted, not only with my heart, but with my most painful secrets. I will probably never know whether they actually believed the rumors or whether they simply didn't have the strength or courage to withstand the pressure from my family and reach their own conclusions, but it matters little. Ultimately, though they shook me deeply, those losses only served to further highlight the inherently abusive nature of my birth family and remind me of the reasons I could no longer be part of it. While I did have a few brief interactions with some of the family members in question in subsequent years, most of them were negative and only served to cement the realization that my journey with my birth family was over. I finally reached a point where I genuinely wished them well and hoped they would find happiness, but had no desire to be part of their lives.

While all of this was playing out with my family, I was also fighting desperately for my health. Even after giving birth, my migraines were worse than ever and my hormone levels were wildly out of control, and despite seeing several specialists, I was not getting any better. Having grown up in a family who believed solely in western medicine, I thought little of seeing doctor after doctor, all of whom prescribed medication to treat my symptoms and then more medications to treat the side effects of those medications. It got to the point where I was so drugged and detached from myself that I could barely remember who or where I was, and life was proceeding without me. Even when the medications gave me enough pain relief to be mildly present, my short-term memory was so affected by the drugs that I could barely recall anything anyway. I remained so seriously ill that I could hardly get out of bed for eighteen months, was hospitalized repeatedly, and came dangerously close to death more than once.

To make matters worse, I had grown so depressed that my visions had turned dark and I was regularly having premonitions of tragedies I could not prevent. It was as if my misery had opened a metaphysical trapdoor into hell and I was suddenly seeing plane crashes, serial murders, and mass casualty events before they happened. Since I felt I couldn't share these visions with anyone and I couldn't prevent any of the horrors I was seeing, I became even more depressed. Soon, I was merely a shadow of myself and grew deeply despondent. For the first time in my life, I struggled with my will to live, finding it only in Joe and our infant son.

No matter how bad things got, Joe took care of me and stayed right by my side, holding my hand through all of it. I have no idea how my amazing husband managed to get through that horrible time, not only taking care of a chronically ill wife, but also taking care of our baby son—all while starting his medical career. I will always be deeply grateful for his strength and his love, as I would not be here without him.

As each well-meaning, but ultimately disengaged doctor chased my every new symptom and side effect with pharmaceuticals, I felt worse and worse and lost more and more of myself. One night, while trying fruitlessly to sleep in an uncomfortable hospital bed after being admitted yet again, I had a vision: I saw the earth as a large globe, spinning in space. Within that globe, I saw newer modalities of health, including large hospital systems, pharmaceutical companies, and surgical suites populate in gray over the United States, Australia, and much of Europe. Then, I saw traditional healing modalities, like wild-grown produce, clean, sparkling water sources, sunlight, herbs, and joyful communities filled with laughter and dancing populate in gold over much of Africa, Central America, and South America. Slowly, the entities in gray dropped into the space below the earth and vibrated with dark, oppressive energy. The entities in gold rose to the space above the earth and vibrated with light, joyful energy. The implication was clear: I needed to choose which vibration I resonated with and wanted to be part of.

In that moment, I finally realized that western medicine was not healing me and was never going to. If I truly wanted to reclaim my health, I had to take full responsibility for it and commit to dealing with the underlying cause of my illness—my lingering trauma. I immediately fired all but one of my doctors, got off all medications, and walked away from all of it. Finally understanding that western medicine was not the answer for me, I got myself a naturopathic and holistic health education, got reacquainted with my own body, did a thorough detox to remove residual drugs and other toxins from my body, removed chemicals from my diet and beauty routine, started eating primarily organic whole foods, resumed regular exercise with an emphasis on weight training, started meditating daily, and spent as much time in nature as possible.

It was slow going at first, but within a matter of weeks, I went from chronically ill and bedridden to being able to take walks, be social, and participate in life again, and within a matter of months, my energy, stamina, and spirit had largely returned and I was finally starting to feel like myself again.

# CHAPTER EIGHT

MY HEALTH WAS FINALLY under control and I was getting better and stronger all the time. I still suffered from migraines, but not nearly to the extent I had before. Though I had been advised by many doctors not to get pregnant again because it nearly killed me the first time, I had since grown much stronger and realized that the combination of unresolved trauma, continuing to put myself in toxic situations, and polluting my body with chemicals was really what had almost killed me. I took complete responsibility for my own health and well-being and was able to carry and give birth to two more beautiful baby boys.

But as my health and happiness were steadily improving, Joe's were steadily declining. Not only had he not yet dealt fully with his abuse and resulting PTSD, but he had also spent the better part of two years having to take care of me and our eldest son. There had been no time or space to take care of anything else, and I was finally healthy and present enough to see just how much my sweet husband was suffering. It seemed like every stressor triggered his disappearing act—and with three small children, there were a *lot* of stressors. The less he was present, the more alone I felt, and our marriage began to fall apart.

Desperate to help his beautiful soul break free from the confines of its captivity, I was determined to find someone who could help him. He had tried therapists and self-help programs like Landmark and Avatar in the past (as had I), and while some of it helped, none of it was nearly enough. I knew we needed someone extraordinary, someone brilliant enough to earn Joe's respect and powerful enough to handle the level of trauma he was dealing with.

Finally, despondent, I confided in a friend about our situation. He said, "I know someone you need to meet." He described an extraordinarily gifted healer, Christopher Maher, with whom he had gone through several years of training in various healing modalities. He told me that Christopher—a former Navy SEAL who had also experienced profound trauma as a child—had created a unique approach to healing that employed a combination of ancient disciplines and modern techniques to free people of every kind of trauma imaginable—including PTSD.

He warned me that his techniques were not run-of-the-mill and suggested I read his book to see what I thought.

I ordered his book that day and eagerly awaited its arrival. When I tore open the package and saw the man on the cover, I felt that familiar tingling in my gut. I immediately hopped online and found a video of him speaking and was struck by the beauty, radiance, and depth of his energy. He was clearly brilliant, strong, and powerful and definitely seemed like the person I was looking for, but I wanted to speak with him before I brought any of this up with my husband. Joe had already been through so much and I did not want to waste his time with someone I wasn't sure about.

I emailed him to set up a phone appointment and as soon as I heard his voice, I knew with absolute certainty that he was the one. Though we were strangers, there was an odd familiarity between us. Our conversation was effortless and flowed as though we had known each other for years. His words and his vibration resonated with me deeply and I trusted that the universe had answered my prayers and brought me exactly who I needed. I told Joe that I had found someone who could help.

My sweet husband, who is highly skeptical by nature, was not excited about this at all, and in fact, was quite resistant to the idea. However, I was insistent, as our relationship was in a very perilous place, and though I loved him more deeply than I had known I could love anyone and truly wanted to make our marriage work, I was afraid that without drastic intervention, we would soon implode. This felt like our last chance. Mercifully, he consented, and shortly thereafter, began his week with Christopher.

When he left for his first session Monday morning, it was clear that he thought it would be a waste of time. But because he is a wonderful, caring man and knew how important it was to me, he went. At this point, I really had no idea what working with Christopher entailed. In truth, since my intuition told me that my search was over when I saw him on the cover of his book, I didn't even read it before I called him (though I did end up reading it a few weeks later after I saw what happened to Joe). So, I had no idea what to expect when Joe came home that evening. When he walked through the door, his mood was not terribly different from usual, but to my great surprise, the dark entity that had been clinging to him since the moment we met seemed to have loosened its grip a bit. It appeared more faded than I had ever seen it, and rather than clinging to Joe like a second skin, it had moved about an inch off of him and was hovering slightly to his right. The next morning, I was delighted to find that he was more present with our children than I had ever seen him, and he seemed to be genuinely enjoying their company.

Each day, there were noticeable improvements. I got to see more and more of the beautiful man I married; he kept coming home happier, more present, more aware, and more loving than the day before. By Wednesday, the shadow entity was no longer hovering near Joe and had moved to his periphery a couple feet away from him. I noticed the whites of his eyes were stunningly bright, like a light had come on inside him. By Friday, the entity was gone altogether and Joe was like a new person, finally free to be his true self, free from all of the negative programming, manipulation, and fear he had been living with.

I was stunned and overjoyed. I had had high hopes, of course, but I don't think I really understood what was possible until I got to experience my husband fully present, right in front of me, free of the trauma and stress that had been sitting between us since the day we met. I had my husband back and our boys had their father back. It was, quite literally, a miracle. I decided I had to meet Christopher in person as I knew I still had work to do, and after seeing Joe's results, I couldn't wait to see what was possible for me. I immediately reached out to Christopher and scheduled my own week with him, eager to rid myself of the trauma and stress that had created so much darkness in my life.

I set off for his beachfront house in Marina del Rey on a Monday morning in February. As my rideshare approached the spot where his address was supposed to be, I didn't see his building number anywhere. There was a building nearby being renovated, covered in scaffolding, which I figured must be hiding the address. As I got out of the car and headed toward the entrance, I saw that there were several construction workers all over the property—including five of them standing right by the lobby. My heart sank; walking through a construction site was always a degrading nightmare for me, as it is for many women I know. I tried to put my head down and barrel through the workers, pretending I didn't hear the catcalls and lewd comments, but one burly guy in particular was determined to be heard. He positioned himself right between me and the front door, looked me up and down excruciatingly slowly, and made a comment that is unfit to preserve in print. Ignoring him, I pushed my way through the entrance, walked up the two flights of stairs to Christopher's floor, and with great anticipation, knocked on his door.

# CHAPTER NINE

WHEN CHRISTOPHER OPENED THE door, we were both rendered speechless and just stared at each other. In reality, the silence probably only lasted for a minute or two, but it seemed like an eternity. Though I had never seen him before except on the cover of his book, I could feel his energy and vibration and he was unquestionably a soul I was deeply familiar with. Somehow, I knew him, and he clearly knew me . . . but I couldn't place him. Finally, I broke the silence and introduced myself, and he invited me inside.

I was taken by the beauty of his office—the beautiful paintings of Isis, Jesus, and other spiritual leaders, an ornate statue of Buddha, vibrant crystal pyramids on every ledge, gentle sunlight streaming through soft, gauzy curtains, and the sweet, cloying smell of palo santo hanging in the air. As I walked down the hall, surveying his artwork, I was stunned to see a giant Egyptian papyrus painting—the very same piece I had bought for myself in Egypt.

Eager to get to work, I shared my story with him, including every painful detail of the sexual assaults I had experienced. He explained to me that because my sexual boundaries were broken early in childhood, my body was essentially acting like a lighthouse, energetically blasting my sexual trauma far and wide for others to pick up on. Even though my mind believed that the last thing I wanted was unwanted sexual attention, my body was actively attracting it, as—whether you are conscious of it or not—you always attract the same frequency you are broadcasting (this is why countless studies show that sexual victimization in childhood or adolescence significantly increases the probability of revictimization in adulthood). So, the first order of business was to transmute those negative energies from my body.

Everything is energy. Energy cannot be destroyed, but it can be changed. Transmutation is an energetic healing practice that transforms low-functioning vibrations, energy, and behavior into high-functioning vibrations, energy, and behavior. To accomplish this, we used a tool he developed called *Body of Light*, which he describes as "a verbal-based energetic system used to help people reintegrate and locate the energies, consciousness, and projections that keep their bodies, brains, and nervous systems out of alignment." As we began this exercise, I did not initially feel a drastic change. It was lovely and soothing, but not earth-shattering . . . until we finished. The second it was over, I was gripped by an intense, immersive vision:

I saw a young woman with long, dark brown hair running across the deck of a ship in the middle of the night. She was being pursued by a stocky blonde man in an ivory linen shirt and breeches, who eventually caught up with her, pinned her up against the railings, and pressed his forearm across her mouth, muzzling her as she tried to scream. The next moment, they were gone, and I was standing in the middle of a forest clearing somewhere in Massachusetts, circa 1760–1780 (I could not pin down the exact year), with an energetic cage around my heart, throat, and third eye. The dark-haired woman was standing right in front of me, smiling at me lovingly, and behind her were rows and rows of other women, varying in age and appearance. I knew they were my ancestors, and that every single one of them had been sexually assaulted, and many had also been stoned to death, burned alive, branded, enslaved, or otherwise tortured, abused, and murdered. I believe the brunette was the first female in my ancestral line to bring her rape trauma to this continent, which is why she showed me her assault. In the forest clearing, she stepped forward, put her hands on my cheeks as a loving mother might, smiled at me, and wrapped me in a tight embrace. As she was holding me, the cage around me dissolved and floated away and I felt a rush of love enter my heart, power filled my throat, and intuition flooded my third eye. All of my other ancestors formed concentric circles around us, hugging each other, with me in the center. As we all embraced, I felt our bodies grow warm with light, and beautiful golden energy filled each of us and created a protective circle around us. One by one, the darkness in each woman dissolved and was replaced by pure, divine love. Waving goodbye, each of them floated away, back up into the heavens, free to resume their soul journeys free of the traumatic trappings of the past, until they were all gone and I was standing alone in the forest.

I was simultaneously overcome by elation, grief, and fulfillment, and felt tears streaming uncontrollably down my face. I realized that the cage around me represents the imprisonment of the Divine Feminine, which has been subjugated, persecuted, and punished for many millennia. The cage's dissolution portends the return of the Divine Feminine, and thus a return to balance and harmony on earth.

As I opened my eyes, I couldn't stop yawning, to the point that I was barely able to relay my vision because I was yawning every three to five seconds! I learned that this is one of the body's many ways of releasing energy (I have seen others hiccup and/or burp compulsively in transmutation). I was immediately reminded of sitting around my dinner table as a child. My parents had my sister and me take turns saying the blessing, and nearly every time it was my turn, I would inexplicably start yawning in the middle of it (this frequently happened in church, as well). This infuriated my parents, who insisted that it was disrespectful to God, and always made me say it over again until I could do it without yawning. I tried to control it, of course, as it was mortifying, and I certainly meant no disrespect, but I simply couldn't help it. In retrospect, I now realize that I was transmuting discordant energy, and that it was not only involuntary, but a gift, rather than the insult they believed it to be.

Quite overwhelmed and exhausted from what I had just experienced, I took a break and ventured out for some sunshine and some lunch. I was too wiped out to take the stairs, so decided to take the elevator. I pressed the button and when the elevator doors opened, I was horrified to see the burly construction worker who had blocked my path on the way in that morning. Groaning inwardly, I briefly considered waiting for the next one, but realized that since the building was under construction, avoiding the workers would be impossible whether I took the elevator or not, and decided to be brave.

I fortified myself for the harassment I knew was forthcoming, but then the strangest thing happened. As the elevator doors closed, the man briefly met my gaze, but as soon as his eyes met mine, he quickly averted them and looked down at the floor. While still staring at the floor, he said in a very soft, nonthreatening voice (quite the opposite of his earlier tone), "Excuse me ma'am, I apologize for bothering you, but I hope you don't mind me saying that you are very beautiful," smiled up at me briefly, and then bowed his head deferentially. I was absolutely stunned, and quite perplexed. He spoke to me as though he had never seen me before in his life, much less a mere two hours earlier. I looked him up and down, thinking perhaps I had confused him with another worker. But no, it was definitely him. Then I wondered whether perhaps he could be bipolar, or whether a large piece of construction equipment had fallen on his head in the short time I had been upstairs. Whatever the cause, his behavior baffled me.

As I walked along the beach in search of a good lunch spot, I couldn't get the incident out of my mind. Finally, I arrived at a festive little Cuban restaurant with a beautiful patio. I grabbed a sidewalk table with a view of the ocean and looked over the menu. Across the patio, I observed a very grumpy waiter (who appeared to be the only one working the patio that day) impatiently answer the questions of an elderly couple, snap at a coworker, and then huffily take the order of a young couple with a baby. As he finally headed my way, I braced myself for his surliness. But when I looked up at him, he hit me with a big, genuine smile, said hello, and asked me—with sincere interest—about my day. I was taken aback by his abrupt change in mood, but happily engaged in conversation with him. Over the course of my meal, he was incredibly kind to me and went out of his way to be attentive: he refilled my water and tea before they dwindled to even two-thirds full, he diligently adjusted my umbrella with every inch the sun moved to keep it out of my eyes, and when a smoker paused briefly on the sidewalk in front of my table, he was quick to hustle him away and apologized to me for the intrusion!

After lunch, as I walked back to Christopher's place, I took a shortcut down a narrow side street and came upon a large group of raucous young men blocking the path. They were loud, boisterous, and obviously drunk. Now, this is the type of situation I would normally avoid like the plague, because in the past, circumstances like this had always resulted in unwelcome harassment—or worse—for me. But as I started to turn back, I heard a voice call, "Excuse us miss, let us get out of your way!" Startled, I turned toward them and saw them moving aside to let me pass. They all smiled at me, several of them removed their hats, and others nodded respectfully. As I tentatively walked through them, I dropped my bag, and three of them simultaneously dashed to pick it up. The man who handed it to me said, "Have a wonderful day ma'am," and smiled at me—without a hint of suggestion, provocation, or indecency. In fact, he was downright gallant.

I was stunned. I had never had the experience of feeling respected, protected, and safe around strange men, much less three times in an hour! What in the world was going on?

This is the very question I asked Christopher upon my return. He explained to me that when we transmuted my sexual trauma, we removed the dark energies that were causing me to unconsciously exhibit a negative frequency and pull negative sexual attention and experiences toward me. This completely and fundamentally changed the way I show up in the world and, as a result, the way other people—especially men—treat me. Instead of being disrespectful, harassing, sadistic, and predatory, they are now reverent, gracious, help-ful, and protective. While I thought I understood the basic concept of transmutation, I had no idea how instantaneous, dramatic, and permanent the results would be. I was starting to understand how Joe had made such incredible strides in just a few days.

That night, I experienced the most violently ill night of my life.

Upon arriving home earlier, I took a long, glorious healing bath in an attempt to recuperate from the intensity of my day. As I soaked in the balmy water, I was overcome with a deeper serenity than I had ever felt. Though I could still easily recall the details of each sexual assault I had transmuted earlier that day, I could no longer feel an emotional charge attached to any of them. Though a mere few hours earlier, those memories had been so painful that I could not recount them without crying, they now felt like they had not even happened to me, like they were incidents I had read about in a novel or heard on the news. I could actually feel the absence of the pain, fear, anxiety, and sadness I had been carrying for years and my notoriously frenzied mind was finally still. I felt truly peaceful for the first time in my memory.

Suddenly, my head was seized by searing pain, as if it were in a vise, and I abruptly vomited into the bathtub. Stunned by the intensity of the pain and confused by its rapid onset,

I tried to stand up and get out of the tub. The room started to spin and I slipped, reaching frantically for the towel bar to catch myself. My vision blurred and I started to feel very hot and feverish. I pulled myself up and over the side of the tub and collapsed onto the floor. And then everything went black.

I woke up on the floor, naked and feverish, in a puddle of my own sweat. My previously dry hair was drenched, each curl clinging to my face like I was in a sweat lodge. The agony in my head was otherworldly—unlike anything I had ever experienced, even at my sickest—and it was unbearable. It felt like heated blades were being pushed slowly into my temples and orbital sockets, and no matter how I twisted and writhed, it only worsened. I was involuntarily sobbing and clutching my head, pulling violently at my hair in an effort to feel anything other than the blinding pain in my head. I felt the nausea welling up again and dragged myself over to the toilet.

I vomited over and over and over for hours, scarcely having a moment to recover before the heaving began again. As convulsions wracked my body, I began having visions. I saw a rapid montage, like the one I saw in Abu Simbel, but this time the images were of my own countless sexual assaults—in this life and many, many others. One after the next, they flashed before my eyes like a movie reel, and though each lasted only a fraction of a second, I felt every violation—every strike, every strangulation, every slash, and every penetration—like it was happening that very moment. As I relived each nightmarish assault, I wondered whether I might be dying, as I felt so very far from earth and so far removed from my body that I wasn't sure I would ever make it back.

But finally, as the darkness of the night began to fade, so did my visions, and I weakly curled my depleted body around the toilet base, my feverish sweating transformed into uncontrollable shivering, and I became extremely cold. Though the thermostat was set to seventy-five degrees, I lay there, my body quaking, freezing on the floor, until the sun came up.

As the agony waned, I realized that I had purged all of the dark sexual assault energy from not only my body, but from my entire ancestral line. Part of me did die on that dark night of the soul; it was the death of my imposter self, the pretender, whose identity was created by the rage, fear, terror, and anguish that I—and so many of my ancestors—experienced. The death of that part of me allowed the birth of my true, authentic self. And as any mother will tell you, birth is never easy, but it is an unquestionably beautiful and worthwhile experience.

In the endless debate of nature v. nurture, prevailing schools of thought have long asserted that people simply are who they are, and that trauma in our ancestry and upbringing has little to do with the choices we make as adults. Even when past trauma is acknowledged as a possible part of the equation, it's often only personal trauma that is considered.

However, the truth is that we are all profoundly affected by our ancestry. When a person experiences trauma, it alters how their body reads their DNA, thus changing the way their genes function. Those epigenetic idiosyncrasies are then passed down to each subsequent generation. In other words, the trauma experienced by our parents and their parents and their parents gets passed down to us, thereby burdening us with stress and pain that we are destined to either resolve or repeat and pass along to our own children—along with all of the additional trauma we have accumulated in our lifetimes. This means that every bit of pain and suffering from violence, abuse, neglect, enslavement, and persecution is carried forward into every new generation until someone in that lineage has the strength, courage, and wherewithal to break the cycle of intergenerational trauma.

This powerful realization fundamentally changed the way I view my parents and my upbringing. In my limited perspective as a child, I believed that they were abusive and unkind because they did not love me. Now, I realize that their unhappiness had nothing to do with me, and in fact long predated me. They inherited their pain from their parents, just like their parents did from theirs. What I perceived as cruel, uncaring behavior was simply them functioning as best they could within the confines of their inherited stress levels.

We are comfortable with the idea of inheriting physical deficiencies from our parents, like sickle cell anemia or alopecia, but most of us don't realize that we also inherit their emotional deficiencies, like a tendency toward violent behavior or susceptibility to sexual abuse. These predispositions dictate the way you respond to certain stimuli, so even when you think you are acting of your own free will, your epigenetics are influencing the way you relate to the world around you. Until you do the work necessary to mend the fragmentations caused by negative conditioning, you are at their mercy, destined to play out the stress patterns you inherited from those who raised you.

When I returned to Christopher's the next day, he used a physical technique called *Ma Xing*, which engages the bladder channel, considered the master channel in Chinese meridian theory. He explained that this channel has access to every aspect of a human being's behavior and thoughts, including their mind, brain, physical being, spiritual energy, and emotional intelligence.

As I lay face down on the floor, he began walking on the backs of my thighs. At first, it was simply uncomfortable; I was surprised at how much tension I was carrying in the backs of my legs and at how tender they were. As he deepened his pressure and quickened his pace, it soon became excruciating. The intensity of the pain was truly impressive and I found myself breathing as deeply and fully as I had while in labor, surrendering to the agony. As I closed my eyes, inhaling and exhaling with the force of hurricane gales, my entire body began to vibrate and get very warm. Energy was racing through me, thundering so loudly in my head that I ceased to hear my own voice. The ever-intensifying vibrations were pulsating so powerfully that my body began to feel like a magnet repelling the ground beneath me. The pressure increased until the energy was throbbing under me and it literally felt like I was being pushed up off of the ground. Curious, I opened my eyes slightly, and to my utter shock, I saw that there was, indeed, about an inch of space between me and the floor. Incredulous, I chalked it up to delirium resulting from the incredible pain I was in, shut my eyes, and resumed breathing with all the fortitude I could muster.

When Christopher finally stepped off of me, I lay there, facedown, barely conscious, with sweat dripping into my eyes. I could not move or speak, and I remained there, motionless, for what felt like an hour. When the pulsating began to subside at last, I finally mustered the strength to lift my head and was surprised to see that he was right there with me, gently holding the space and waiting for me to recover. I turned to him and asked, "I feel crazy even asking this question, but I have to know—was my imagination playing tricks on me, or was I actually levitating?" And he replied, "Why do you think I was standing on you?" and winked.

We continued our work all week, using combinations of *Ma Xing*, *Body of Light*, and destressing and detensing body work techniques that involve isometric, concentric, and eccentric contractions. With every session, I had astonishing experiences and revelations that changed my perspective. As we continued to peel away layer after layer of stress and trauma, I felt eminently lighter, brighter, and more joyful. The unremitting level of anxiety and stress I had learned to live with as a child and operate through as an adult melted away and I began to feel my true self peeking through. I felt space and peace in my center where there used to be an ever-present ball of angst, terror, and rage. I felt like I could finally breathe.

At the end of the week, as I wrapped my arms around him in gratitude, something electric raced through me like a lightning bolt and suddenly a familiar image burst into my consciousness. I realized why I had recognized Christopher the moment he opened the door—he was the presence sitting next to me in my visions of Karnak in Ancient Egypt.

# CHAPTER TEN

THE LESSONS I LEARNED and the skills I gained working with Christopher immediately started creating miracles in my daily life. In the days after our work concluded, I noticed myself experiencing emotions with the passion, intensity, and depth I had as a little girl, before I shut my feelings down to protect myself. It felt like a thick layer of armor had dissolved, allowing more and more of my true nature to shine through. I was no longer afraid to feel things, and more importantly, I was no longer afraid to let others see how I felt.

The fear-based paralysis I used to experience on a daily basis, especially regarding my interactions with men and my ability to be authentic, simply disappeared. I continued to have frequent, amazing interactions with strangers who went out of their way to be respectful, thoughtful, and deferential toward me; people couldn't be kind or helpful enough! Before transmuting my trauma, I felt like a beacon for harassment, like I was wearing a sign that said PLEASE MESS WITH ME and was constantly the target of unwanted attention. Now, everywhere I went, I was treated like a queen. I recall taking a walk through the Santa Monica Promenade, which is always packed with people trying to sell things and get petition signatures. Previously, I couldn't make it five feet down the sidewalk before I'd have people in my face, vying for my attention. This time, though I walked the entire length of the promenade and must have passed at least twenty people who were out there hustling for signatures and sales, not *one* person approached me, hollered at me, or encroached on my personal space. In fact, they literally moved aside when I walked by, and many smiled or nodded respectfully—but nobody bothered me. It was as if I had an invisible force field around me that filtered out everything that did not serve me.

I noticed that I was suddenly able to communicate with extreme clarity and grace under any circumstances and was unshaken by the negative behavior of others. One day, Joe and I found ourselves the targets of a nasty, unprovoked tirade by the homeowners association president of our building. This man had a severe inferiority complex, was quite self-loathing and fearful, and was in the habit of taking it out on others (he fined residents for having flowers on their balconies, regularly made obnoxious comments about various races and religions, and even swore at our small children one day for making too much noise outside—on a Saturday afternoon). On this occasion, he threw a tantrum because our furniture delivery men showed up early and brought our couch into the building without his permission. This man got right up in our faces, huffing and puffing, yelling and screaming obscenities, and turning beet red like an angry cartoon character. Previously, when confronted by someone like that, I would have either frozen up entirely and been unable to speak or had a completely outsized reaction containing months or years of sublimated anger that I had been unable to express in a more appropriate time or manner, and verbally eviscerated the party in question. This time, however, neither of those things happened. I remained entirely composed—inside and out—and experienced no stomach flutters, no panic, no dread, no anxiety, no tightening, no seizing up, and no guilt. Instead, I calmly but very firmly spoke to him about the inappropriateness of behaving so poorly in any situation, for any reason. He instantly quieted, backed out of my space, and did not say another word. He also never bothered me, or even met my gaze, again. Thanks to my work with Christopher, my fear was absent and my grace was present.

Physically, I started experiencing drastically increased flexibility, agility, strength, and endurance and I noticed that my hair and nails started growing incredibly fast. Everyone I knew was asking me what I had done to my skin, as getting rid of all that stress took years off my face. Cuts and bruises began healing in record time and I was working out twice as hard and recovering in half the time.

My relationship with the divine felt clearer and more magical than ever. My visions became even more frequent, more detailed, and more beautiful—and started occurring as often in my waking state as my sleeping state. I was able to identify and consciously communicate with many of the divine presences I had always felt, including Archangel Michael, Mary Magdalene, and several other beings of light. I learned that the repetitive numerical patterns I had seen all my life, particularly after meeting Joe, were angelic messages of love, light, and support.

But of all the lessons I learned from my experience with Christopher, the most profoundly important is that everything in my life—and yours—is a co-creation. Contrary to what we are taught, things do not "just happen" to us, and we are not victims of circumstance. Rather, we choose the lessons we wish to learn before we ever incarnate on earth, and once we arrive, our energy collaborates with the energy of others to create the circumstances needed to support us in learning those lessons. In other words, we seek out the experiences we need in order to achieve a new level of soul growth. Despite the fact that each of us arrives here with a predetermined soul contract, we all have free will on the earth plane. So, the path you take once you get here is your choice. While you are provided with the tools and guidance you need on your chosen journey, as well as every opportunity for success, whether or not you fulfill the covenant you created is ultimately your choice. Therefore, I am entirely responsible for my own experience of life—and so are you.

For me, this means that I *chose* to incarnate into an unhappy family, because that situation best supported the lessons my soul was seeking this time around—namely, to learn to trust my own intuition, stand powerfully in my own truth, and embrace my light no matter what the circumstances. If I had been born into a happy, loving, supportive family, I would never have learned to withstand external stressors and influences and think for myself, and would easily have fallen prey to the insidious narratives of control that created the world we live in today.

Moreover, the souls incarnated as my parents did me a great service by playing the role of villains in my journey. I am supremely grateful to them for volunteering for such a difficult job, because their support allowed my soul to experience the growth and development that I wanted. So often, we are taught that we are victims of bad luck or evil intention, but the truth is that we experience the circumstances we need—and have, in fact, energetically invited—in order to fulfill the contract we created. Nothing is an accident; you are always going to see your vibration reflected back to you in some way, shape, or form. Everything we experience in our lives, good or bad, is, on some level, our choice. In my case, this includes not only my difficult childhood, but the sexual assaults, the life-threatening illness, the family separation, and of course, all of the positive experiences including my spectacular husband, our beautiful children, and my illuminating travels.

It can be extremely difficult to resolve the horrific circumstances of people's lives with the notion that they chose to experience it. For me, this is a particularly tall order when it comes to children, who are the purest, most beautiful examples of divinity on earth, and unequivocally my Achilles' heel. Everything in my soul wants to protect children from harm at all costs, and I have spent much of my life in service of that goal. At first, the mere suggestion that the abuse or murder of a precious child could be anything more than an act of evil enraged me. But then I realized two things.

First, I realized that children—sweet little balls of joy though they are—are also boundless, infinite beings just like adults. Their diminutive bodies and adorable natures distract us from the realization that, outside this realm, they too are fully developed souls with as much right to choose their journeys as we have. Second, I realized that many of us choose lives of sacrifice in order to increase the human collective's awareness of and put an end to destructive behaviors on earth. For example, in another persistent vision that I have had since I was a little girl, I am a young mother bound to a stake somewhere in Europe, condemned to be burned alive (for reasons that are unclear). Right next to me are my three daughters, roughly fifteen, eleven, and nine years old, each tied to a stake of her own. A man approaches my daughters with a torch, lighting each of them on fire so that I am forced to watch my children burn before I die. This horrific vision disturbed me deeply for many years. It wasn't until after I transmuted my trauma that I was able to see more of the vision, as well as recover the deep soul memory that I chose to sacrifice myself in that specific way in order to highlight the atrocity of that practice and encourage its retirement—and so did the souls incarnated as my daughters.

As infinite beings having a temporary physical experience, we are not hapless pawns, as we are led to believe, but powerful creators here to play, learn, and grow. Our souls are willing to experience *anything* for the sake of growth—no matter how horrible it may seem to our human minds. "Good" and "bad" are human constructs that we employ on Earth as a way of understanding the world, but our souls do not make these distinctions. To the soul, everything is merely experience and all experience creates growth. In other words, what seems to us like a horrible death or tragedy may be another soul's act of sacrifice and love.

Without the invaluable lessons I learned from my parents, I would never have developed the vision to see clearly through nebulous agendas, the courage to speak the truth to our culture of dishonesty, and the strength to stand unwaveringly for what is right, no matter the cost. And thank goodness, because one week after I finished my last session with

Christopher—in a feat of timing that can only be described as divine—the COVID-19 pandemic began.

When news of the pandemic first began to surface, I was very uneasy; I knew, deep in my gut, that something wasn't right. I could feel dark energy and nefarious intention behind the emerging narrative, but I hadn't yet deduced exactly what was happening. Then, when the lockdowns started, I knew without question that this so-called "pandemic" was not a naturally occurring calamity, as we were being led to believe, but an evil construct designed to frighten the masses into relinquishing their power and sovereignty to a small group of tyrannical elitists.

At the time, our eldest son was in first grade and our middle son was in preschool, so when Joe and I learned that the schools were shutting down—ostensibly for two weeks—we panicked. He was working full time doing research and caring for patients in the hospital, and I was doing my best to work from home while caring for our baby full time. We had no idea how we were going to make it all work.

But, as two weeks stretched into two months—and ultimately, two years—we found ourselves loving the experience of spending so much time together as a family. Though we had always prioritized our family time (or so we believed), it wasn't until the lockdowns happened that we realized how busy we actually were and how much of each day we were spending apart. With Joe at the hospital or the office all day, Eric and Jack in two different schools, and little Max and me at home, the five of us really only saw each other early in the mornings before school started and late in the afternoons after work ended. The disruption of quarantining turned out to be a welcome blessing for us, and we quickly settled into a new routine that focused more on family fun than function.

Thanks to our work with Christopher, Joe and I were doing amazingly well. Our renewed relationship was stronger, more intimate, and more joyful than ever, and we were purposeful partners in every sense. Weeks earlier, the stress of circumstances like these would have devastated what was left of our relationship, but now, we were truly enjoying every moment with each other and with our boys. While he still had to go into the hospital to care for patients from time to time, we were largely home together and made a daily practice of seeing what kind of joy and beauty we could create for our boys using things we already had in the house. We had daily dance parties, cooking classes, Spanish language practice, story time, drawing classes, music appreciation, and art projects. We had weekly theme days, where the boys would draw the name of a state or country out of a jar and we would create a whole day of fun based on the traditions of that place; we cooked and ate their native dishes, learned their native dances, listened to their native music, did their native crafts, studied their people and culture, and watched related movies or film clips.

When Los Angeles schools "reopened" with virtual class-rooms, we thought it was ludicrous to expect small children to have a worthwhile educational experience by sitting in front of a computer screen for several hours a day (remember all the years prior to the pandemic when the American Academy of Pediatrics discouraged any screen time for children under two years old and recommended limiting older children's screen time to no more than an hour or two a day?), so we began homeschooling our boys. Though it was initially a choice we made out of necessity, the absence of schedule and structure turned out to be the best thing that could have happened to our family. We got to spend our days playing, learning, and exploring together and watching the natural curiosity and brilliance of our children come to life. We already knew our boys were incredibly talented, generous, and beautiful souls, but it was truly a gift getting to spend every day discovering their natural talents and affinities. The initial inconvenience of the situation quickly paled in comparison to the blessings it brought, and Joe and I often marveled at the fact that it took a pandemic hitting pause on the whole world to give our kids the kind of childhood we had always wanted them to have.

Though we were largely surrounded by panicking, fearful people, we strived to maintain a peaceful, sane environment at all times, knowing that our reaction to the lockdown would dictate our children's reaction to the lockdown. We were very aware that how we chose to handle the situation would be the difference between our boys thriving and remembering the lockdown as the best, most fun-filled years of their early lives or descending into depression and fear and becoming sad, withdrawn shadows of themselves.

In service of that goal, we kept things as normal and tranquil as possible. Despite the lunacy of local government attempting to lock down the great outdoors (which is no one's right), we spent tons of time outside. We spent hours at the park every day during the week, and on weekends we explored local beaches, mountains, and deserts. When the city cordoned off all the playgrounds and removed all the basketball hoops, we brought sporting equipment to the park and hosted games for local kids. We became fast friends with other families who shared our values and were unwilling to let fear and darkness destroy their children's innocence and joy. Our "freedom crew" had frequent picnics, barbecues, and beach parties and celebrated every birthday and holiday as a community. In spite of the dismal circumstances, we had a magical, marvelous time together—and our kids got to have a childhood.

Every time we were out with the boys, people asked us how and why our kids were so happy under the circumstances and what our secret was. It was gratifying because, though intellectually, I already knew how crucial our stability and well-being was to theirs, it was both humbling and reassuring to see that truth reflected back to us in real time. But it was also heartbreaking, as it became readily apparent that many parents were struggling deeply and their struggles were translating into their children's suffering.

While I empathized deeply with those who were suffering, I was also angered by the insidiousness of the forces working to rob people of their joy, empathy, and compassion. The ability to love and connect is humanity's greatest strength, so preventing us from hugging or touching each other, banning us from socializing with our loved ones, and forcing us to cover our faces could never be in our best interest—and I was struck by how many people did not see that. Rather than trusting their intuition and honoring their true nature, too many people were trusting sinister forces who were clearly trying to take advantage of their compassion by weaponizing false morality. The more dubious "data" came to light, the less sense any of the pandemic response made, yet the masses were all too eager to absorb the steady supply of propaganda being disseminated by the media, the government, and far too much of the medical community.

Joe and I were both profoundly disturbed by the obviously false narrative being pushed on the public, as well as the suspect medical advice being circulated. Between us, we had the benefits of a medical education, an acute understanding of research methods, strong spiritual clarity, and the ability to accurately read other people, so we could easily see through this malicious agenda-pushing. But we were very concerned about everyone who did not have these tools at their disposal and were falling prey to dangerous rhetoric. What about those not familiar enough with medical science to know that natural immunity is an incontrovertible truth? What about those not well-versed enough in research methodology to identify the highly suspect conclusions drawn from poorly designed studies of mask-wearing, when years of clinical trials had found little or no benefit? What about those who never learned to trust their inner voice and are, in fact, so disconnected from themselves that they cannot even hear it? What about those who cannot easily discern the intentions of others and thus don't know who to trust? We knew we had to find a way to help.

Since we'd started homeschooling, Joe and I had very little time alone together. So we started having weekly lunch dates every Tuesday where we would pick up takeout from one of our favorite restaurants (since nothing was open for dine-in business yet), take it to the beach, and have a picnic while we talked about the latest pandemic developments and shared our thoughts and observations. We were both disgusted by the cheap fear tactics, misrepresented data, and logical inconsistencies that were dominating the news cycles, and frustrated by the fact that almost no one seemed to be speaking out against the clearly corrupt narrative. We decided it was time to push back. Over the next several months, our conversations turned into a series of articles offering a different perspective on the pandemic, published in *USA Today* and *The Wall Street Journal*, which Joe wrote and I edited.

The backlash came immediately. Friends and strangers alike came out of the woodwork, infuriated by the mere suggestion that perhaps succumbing to fear and ignoring hard data was not the way to handle the pandemic. The amount of rage and terror aimed at us was surprising (and almost comical, given the fact that we were among a very tiny percentage of voices in the media not lying our asses off for personal gain, and were in fact risking a great deal in an effort to help others). We had friends and colleagues we had known for twenty years suddenly decide that we were insane and evil—merely for questioning the logic of attempting to outrun an airborne respiratory virus with over a 99 percent survival rate by robbing citizens of their civil rights and basic tenets of health. Many of these people were highly intelligent, highly respected leaders in their fields, and it was very difficult for me to reconcile their academic brilliance with their abject failure to recognize that they were being manipulated in service of a powerful agenda that had nothing to do with health.

We watched as our society slipped into a state of mass psychosis far more dangerous than COVID-19 could ever be. I had often wondered as a child how a population could ever reach the level of indoctrination and collective detachment required to allow atrocities like the Holocaust and the Salem witch trials to occur, and now I was witnessing it in real time—the very same dangerous descent into mass delusions and paranoia that had allowed the rise of every past totalitarian regime. Though it was deeply disheartening, Joe and I were unyielding in our efforts, as we were certain that we were acting in the best interest of humanity.

Although we faced intense opposition at seemingly every turn, our intense spiritual work had given Joe and me a new level of freedom around challenge and confrontation, so we remained resolute and unflappable. Additionally, the polarizing nature of our position made it easy to find our tribe, and we were soon forming wonderful new friendships and creating powerful new alliances all over the world.

Unbeknownst to us at the time, Florida governor Ron DeSantis was looking for a new state surgeon general and our articles had caught his team's attention. One afternoon, I came home to find my sweet husband standing in the kitchen with an odd look on his face. When I asked him what was going on, he told me that he had received a call from the governor's office—and they had asked him to accept the position. Though we had just moved into a beautiful new house two weeks earlier and hadn't even finished unpacking yet, my gut lit up with that warm, familiar tingling. This was a perfect opportunity to bring hope and create meaningful change on a large platform, and I knew we had to go for it. So Joe accepted the position, we started putting our freshly unpacked belongings back in boxes, and we said bittersweet goodbyes to our wonderful community.

As we prepared to leave Los Angeles, I reflected on all the ways the pandemic actually served humankind. Though the lockdown was tedious and challenging in many ways, it helped people to clarify their values, prioritize what was actually important to them, and examine their life choices.

It revealed the ugly underbelly of abuse, deception, and manipulation that has plagued our society for generations, lurking in the shadows just out of the public eye. It helped energize a return to the lost values of love, community, and stewardship.

On a personal level, it stripped away all of the external stimuli that I previously relied on to give me false enthusiasm, energy, and significance. In the absence of those stimuli, I was forced to look entirely within, be brutally honest with myself, and rely on my spiritual fortitude to find joy, excitement, and purpose in the world. It was also a great litmus test for my newfound emotional freedom. Though I was surrounded every day by the intense anxiety, frustration, and aggression of the people around me, I absorbed none of it; their fear did not disrupt my vibration at all. Even a month earlier, I would have imploded under this level of exposure to other people's emotional stress. Transmuting my own fear and emotional stress gave me the ability to be a neutral observer during the upheaval, rather than a miserable participant—and the former is an infinitely more powerful position.

In their rush to scare us, dehumanize us, mask us, quarantine us, separate us, control us, and rob us of our empathy, the tyrannical architects of the pandemic have only succeeded in mobilizing lion-hearted humanitarians, ensuring that we find each other, form communities, and powerfully expand our energy until this revolution of love awakens all beings and leaves only light where there once was darkness.

By participating in the narrative of those who seek to control you, you are creating your own prison; you cannot be enslaved without your full consent. There is no authority in which you should put more faith than your own intuition. Stop looking to external sources for answers to life's difficult questions; you already know what is right and true for you. If you are not yet emotionally clear enough to access that truth, then you need to deal with your fear—and that means you first have to deal with the trauma that created it.

# CHAPTER ELEVEN

How DO YOU RID yourself permanently of fear, shame, judgment, and pain? How do you access your true purpose and find the courage to pursue it fearlessly? How do you heal your lineage and free future generations from the trappings of inherited trauma?

Healing yourself—and your lineage—starts with shedding behavioral patterns and limiting beliefs that no longer serve you or the collective consciousness. We all inherit the beliefs and stress patterns of our parents and grandparents, but as our level of consciousness rises, we realize that, though they did the best they could at the time, their methods of parenting and living were not necessarily constructive for us or for humanity. It is our duty to recognize that destructive patterns of behavior like domestic violence, addictions, unhealthy eating habits, and sedentary lifestyles are no longer acceptable and that the dark energies associated with such behavior cannot survive as we collectively raise our vibration.

This is the lifetime many of us have chosen to heal our lineage. Every being that is currently here on Earth is a multidimensional, immortal soul—inviolate and independent, yet inseparably interconnected with all other beings. We each have unique, specific gifts designed to aid the human collective as we create new values, new governing bodies, and a more conscious way of living. Our task is to create a society that works for everyone—not just an elite few—and to achieve that, each of us must take responsibility for our co-creations and our energy and work daily to raise our vibration.

So, how do we do that?

## Practice Self-Love

For many of us—especially those of us who value being of service to others—the term "self-love" makes us uncomfortable. We confuse acts of self-love and self-care with being selfish, but this couldn't be further from the truth. Self-love is not selfish; it is absolutely necessary.

There is the obvious argument that you cannot work endlessly to be of service to others while ignoring your own needs, as you will eventually crash and cease to be useful to anyone. But the larger issue is that our goal as a human collective is to create a just, unified world that works for everyone—and you simply cannot move into loving unity consciousness while leaving yourself out. It is not possible to make real strides toward a new, divine society if you are busy denying yourself the care you need in order to be the best, fullest, highest-vibrational version of yourself.

Even as I write this, I am still very much practicing this skill and learning to embody it in my daily life. As a wife, mother, healer, and teacher, I am far more comfortable with and accustomed to taking care of others. I am not alone in this, as people who have not yet learned to value themselves often eat poorly, exercise infrequently, isolate from others, and participate in activities or spend time with people who are bad for them—thinking they don't have a choice. But after spending years sacrificing my needs and my health in an ill-fated attempt to please others, I have learned the hard way that we ignore our well-being at our own peril.

So let us move out of perpetual self-sacrifice and self-neglect and prioritize self-love and self-care. Make a conscious decision each day to do as many kind things for yourself as you can. Make time to do things that fill your heart with joy! Dance, sing, swim, skip, cook, craft, run, twirl, read, write, travel, and play. Believe that you are deserving of love, joy, adventure, and beauty, because the only person who can give you the fulfillment and the approval you long for is you.

## Balance Giving and Receiving

This is an extension of self-love. Many of us—particularly those of us with strong service missions—are much more comfortable giving than receiving. Some have been taught that it is better to give than receive, some have been taught that receiving takes away from another, some have been conditioned not to expect assistance because they come from backgrounds where their needs were not met, and some believe that receiving help comes with obligations or will make others dislike or distrust you. However, all of these limiting beliefs are based in fear.

The truth is that an equal balance of giving and receiving creates natural harmony and flow. Imagine how wonderful it feels when you are able to give someone something they genuinely want or truly need. When you refuse to receive, you are denying another that same joy. Allowing yourself to graciously receive helps you be of service to others—and sometimes your highest service is to allow others to give.

If you have difficulty receiving because you are uncomfortable with the idea of owing another, practice setting your intention to receive from Source, rather than from other people. If you choose to view individuals who give you time, love, energy, money, goods, or wisdom as conduits of divine orchestration, you can be a willing participant in the exchange and welcome the balance of giving and receiving.

Some are more comfortable receiving than giving. Often this stems from the belief that resources, including time, money, love, and energy are limited. But love and energy are abundant, limitless resources—give them freely! Let go of the limiting beliefs that you do not have enough to go around or might run out if you give too much. Further, let go of the limiting belief that you cannot give to strangers or to those you do not like or cannot relate to. Adopt the perspective that you are generous, you are powerful, you are abundant, you are fulfilled, you have more than enough, and you can easily give to others.

Giving can take many forms, so be of service in whatever way feels right for you. What do you have to give? If you are athletic, start a sports league for inner-city kids. If you are a gifted gardener, share fresh produce with your colleagues. If you are a talented chef, make meals for your elderly neighbors. If you are wealthy, financially support a humanitarian cause that touches your heart. If you are able-bodied, shovel the snowy driveway of a wheelchair-bound friend. If you are artistic, help the theater department at a local school create production backdrops. Each of us is blessed with unique gifts and talents; use them to enrich your community and bless the lives of others.

## Speak with Honesty, Clarity, and Vulnerability

One of the primary reasons our society has descended into narcissism, hostility, and violence is because at some point, alleged leaders started prioritizing profit and control over honesty and truth. Government has become synonymous with greed, obfuscation, manipulation, and dishonesty. The leaders our world needs most are leaders with a willingness to be vulnerable and speak honestly about their emotions. It is a great service to be emotionally honest and vulnerable, as it lets others know that they are not alone and that there is a way out of the pain they are in. When you share your stories and tell others about the emotional struggles you have faced, you give others permission to do the same.

The constant propaganda disseminated during the pandemic made me realize what a powerful thing it is to share your truth with no expectations or investment in the outcome. When you speak authentically and without agenda, others respond to that energy—whether they want to or not—because it stands in stark contrast to the vast majority of messaging that surrounds us every day and is thus quite arresting.

And it is not merely what you say; *how* you speak is also important. Communicate clearly and truthfully using powerful, expressive language. Honor yourself and those with whom you are communicating by ridding your vocabulary of modifiers that diminish your power. Many of us (myself included) are prone to modifying our statements in order to appear less objectionable. For example, you might say, "It kind of bothers me a little when you don't really look at me when I am talking to you," when the more direct, truthful, and powerful statement is, "It bothers me when you don't look at me when I am talking to you." Do not diminish your words in order to rescue others from their discomfort. Say what you mean and say it kindly and directly. As a society, it has become acceptable to speak with little to no integrity, and this serves no one. Be courageous, be clear, and be *you*.

## Consume Consciously

Everything you consume—including food, drinks, substances, television, radio, podcasts, news, social media, and even the energy of others—affects your vibration. Each choice you make will either raise it or lower it. This may be an intimidating realization, but it is also a powerful one; you are in control over what you consume, therefore you are in control of your vibration. What are you choosing to put into your body and soul every day?

Many are awakening to the realization that humans have been controlled for ages by an elite, concealed group of dark actors who have a keen interest in keeping humanity's collective vibration low so that we can be more easily manipulated. They use many different methods and tools of control, but the most insidiously effective are those that appear most innocuous—like food and water.

It is a basic human right—not to mention a divine right—to have access to clean, healthy food and water. After all, we cannot thrive, or even survive, without both. Clean water is the basis for all life, growth, and cleansing, and clean nutrition is how we keep our body strong and healthy and defend against illness. It is obviously problematic and unjust when populations lose their access to food and water altogether, and this tends to mobilize humanitarians who wish to help. A less obvious, but equally malicious strategy is to allow humans all the access they want, but poison the supply.

Through the aggressive use of chemical pesticides, herbicides, hormone disrupters, and antibiotics, and the advent of genetically modified organisms (GMOs), our food can do us more harm than good. We know these substances increase the risk of cancer, infertility, immune problems (among several other conditions)—and they lower your vibration. This is also true of our tap water supply, which has been pumped full of contaminants, including fluoride, chorine, lead, volatile organic compounds (VOCs), and mercury—all of which cause health problems and, you guessed it, lower your vibration.

It is critical not just to your physical well-being but to your spiritual well-being that you nourish your body with clean foods and water. Whenever possible, choose fresh, local, and organic foods. Buy from farmer's markets instead of grocery stores, and if you have the space (even a windowsill will do!), start a little garden and grow your own. Avoid GMOs at all costs. Filter your drinking water, and if possible, filter the water you cook and shower with as well.

Other substances that lower your vibration include alcohol, caffeine, pharmaceutical and recreational drugs, theobromine (found in chocolate), nicotine, and refined sugars. All of these chemical concoctions disassociate you from your mind, body, and soul and provide an artificial means of regulating your hormones and stimulating your mood—and they are all addictive. They provide a false high and a lower vibration.

I have relied on several of these substances in the past, and for a long time, had no idea they were problematic. It wasn't until I shed my trauma that my vibration really started to rise and I could actively feel when something disrupted it. I truly thought I would have the hardest time giving up caffeine and the easiest time giving up sugar and chocolate because I didn't use them that much and thought our relationship was casual . . . WRONG! Upon self-examination, I realized that my addictive relationship to caffeine stemmed from my constant need to always be "on" and perform at a very high level, because I didn't know who I was if I wasn't achieving something. Much of that hang-up naturally dissolved as a result of transmuting my trauma, so the only pain involved in giving up caffeine was physical. Conversely, my attachments to chocolate and sugar were far more complicated and difficult to release, in that they were emotional; I was using them to mask my sadness and make myself feel better in lieu of actually doing the spiritual work to raise my vibration.

Giving them up wasn't easy, but it was worth it. Every day I choose not to ingest these substances I feel stronger, clearer, calmer, happier, more aligned with the divine, and more inspired to make healthy choices that honor who I really am and support my growth rather than hinder it. I also experienced my physical body performing at a much higher level than it used to and hitting milestones approximately four to five times faster than I was before. As a lifelong athlete, it's ironic that I started using caffeine very early to boost my physical fitness and performance, but since I stopped using it, I am stronger and faster than ever.

During the pandemic, I noticed a sudden influx of billboards advertising the availability and delivery of various alcohol and marijuana products. While many celebrated the convenience of being able to get your drug of choice delivered to your home in the middle of lockdowns, I saw a treacherous, calculated attempt to lower the vibration of the population *en masse*.

The irony is that the high available from raising your vibration and being in spiritual alignment with the divine is far better, cleaner, and more blissful than any drug-induced, man-made high could ever be. Believe me—by the lowest point in my illness, I was on a plethora of mind and mood-altering pharmaceuticals, and after the initial drug-induced euphoria, all I ever felt was numb and dissociated. In the moments I have reached a true vibrational high—including my many soul-awakening experiences in Egypt and with Christopher— the euphoria has been so pure, so intense, and so all-consuming that I have often wished I could go back in time and tell my younger self that using agents of disconnection to deal with pain is not worth it.

It is not only consumption of food, drink, and drugs that affects you; everything you watch, read, and listen to also has a vibration and will absolutely affect yours. Be mindful of what you allow into your mind, body, and soul. Be discerning about where you choose to get your information and consider the integrity of the source. For example, instead of watching a horror movie, consider watching a comedy or nature documentary that interests you. Instead of reading celebrity gossip magazines, consider reading a biography of someone you admire. Instead of listening to angry death metal, consider listening to enchanting, ethereal music. Instead of watching mindless pranks on social media, consider watching a guided meditation or a how-to video.

Limit your consumption of mainstream media. It is clear to anyone looking with open eyes—regardless of political or religious affiliation—that the media is merely a propaganda vehicle at this point. Since 90 percent of mainstream media in the United States is owned by only six corporations, all with a vested interest in convincing the population to believe the narrative that keeps them in power, there is little, if any, actual news being reported. Today, the media exists solely to create fear, separation, racism, sexism, misogyny, xenophobia, and general distrust of other human beings.

If you are going to consume any media, you must judiciously consider the source and do your own corroborating research before accepting anything you read, hear, or see as truth. It is not an exaggeration to say that the COVID-19 pandemic and its resulting policies would not exist without the media. They are directly responsible for spreading lies and distrust of others with the clear intention of creating fear and panic.

The media is also responsible for the creation of "wokeness" and "cancel culture." By constantly manipulating humans to focus on our superficial differences rather than our myriad similarities, the media creates distraction and hostility. Worse, by encouraging us to immediately dismiss anything that makes us uncomfortable or that we disagree with rather than having an honest conversation about it, they create a tribal, polarized world in which everyone must pick a side or be relegated to the fringes of our society. None of this serves humanity—but it certainly serves those who seek to control or destroy it. The truth they so desperately seek to obscure is that we are all one. Regardless of race, religion, sexual orientation, socioeconomic status, or anything else, we are all beings of one shared consciousness seeking the same things: love, light, health, joy, and purpose. Can you imagine the great healing that would take place if only we focused our energy on everything we have in common, rather than allowing ourselves to be morally manipulated by our trivial differences?

Like mainstream media, social media is also designed to create distraction, sow discord, cause infighting, obscure intuition, and discourage critical thinking. It also encourages far too much time spent creating a false sense of connection and intimacy behind a computer screen, and—by targeting users with content designed to appeal specifically to them—distorts our perception of the world. It is also designed to create addiction by stimulating the production of dopamine and other neurotransmitters in the brain. As a result, the more time we spend online engaged in a false reality, the less time we spend in the real world developing real relationships with real people and making real contributions.

Additionally, social media has spawned the so-called vocation of "influencers," an entire profession devoted solely to people—often young and attractive—telling others what they should want and need. Since our collective evolution wholly depends on each of us learning to look inward, trust our gut, and follow our own path, it is brilliantly underhanded—and no surprise—that those who seek to control us would create an entire industry designed to lure us away from our intuition. Our growth as a species requires that each of us reclaim our sovereignty, realize our true power as reflections of the divine, and make our own choices about what is right for us. Beware the superficial blather of those being paid to encourage consumerism and tell others what is best for them. No one knows what's best for you except *you*.

On that note, it is also worth exercising caution with alternative and enlightened news sources. Though the misinformation surrounding the pandemic catalyzed the development of numerous alternative news sources—many of them excellently written and discerning—that doesn't necessarily mean that it is in your best interest to consume them. Even if they deliver credible information that is well-intentioned and designed to inform, that information may not necessarily elevate your consciousness and could serve to further distract you from listening to your intuition about any given circumstance.

Early in the pandemic, I fell victim to this trap myself. From the start, my intuition was clearly telling me that COVID-19 was a manufactured virus created to justify the emergency use of control mechanisms on the population, but very few people in my life shared my view at that point. Desperate to corroborate the suspicions plaguing me, I did an incredible amount of research and absorbed an abundance of information from well-intentioned whistleblowers, doctors, nurses, scientists, etc. While enlightening and reassuring, I quickly realized that most of this information only served to excite and titillate—just like mainstream media. It did not raise my vibration at all, and in fact, lowered it by keeping me a prisoner to external resources and giving me a convenient excuse to keep looking outward rather than inward—which is where the answers I sought truly lie.

Before you consume anything, ask yourself what effect it is likely to have on your vibration, and before you share with anyone else, ask what effect it is likely to have on theirs.

## Choose Divine Relationships

We choose every relationship in our lives—starting with the families we are born into. Many of us, like myself, chose to experience victim consciousness in this life for the purpose of triggering an awakening that would ultimately help humanity end the cycle of pain and suffering it has been experiencing for millennia. We chose the experience of feeling powerless so that we were forced to remember that we are, in actuality, quite powerful. In other words, we incarnate into the families we need so that we can experience the growth we want.

This is often an extremely painful experience; if it were not, we would not experience the intended spiritual evolution and subsequently devote our lives to helping humanity grow beyond its current limitations. This path frequently results in difficult, fractured familial relationships, and many of us ultimately choose to leave home and family in search of our true selves.

But, as I learned (or, more accurately, remembered) after transmuting much of my trauma, the members of my family also chose their family experiences before incarnating, meaning they volunteered to play their respective roles in my life for the purpose of triggering my reawakening. Without them, I would never have had reason or opportunity to recall ancient memories of the trauma I experienced in other lifetimes—as well as the trauma experienced by the human collective—and I would never had been able to transmute it, recover my true self, and contribute to the overall awakening of humanity. Thus, I am grateful to my family for granting me this experience.

However cruel, unkind, or uncaring your birth family's behavior may be, the nature of their souls is generous and divine. Though likely not conscious, their beliefs and behaviors are unquestionably supporting you on your soul's journey by motivating you to grow spiritually. It is not your right or responsibility to judge the nature of their journeys or change what they believe. Every soul has the divine right to pursue enlightenment at the pace they choose, and you must honor their choices—but you don't have to stay in an abusive situation.

Unconditional love requires letting go of the need to control the circumstances of another or please others at the cost of your own peace. Inescapably torn between the desire to please our families and the need to fulfill our deep, inner purpose, we often tell ourselves that we cannot stand up to loved ones because it will hurt their feelings, or that we cannot walk away from an abusive situation because love means tolerating anything and everything. The notion that being loving means we don't rock the boat is a lie we tell ourselves in order to diminish our power. Love is strong, radiant, and courageous; it requires that you stand up, be your true self, and step masterfully into your power. Not only is this the right thing to do for yourself, but by honoring your true nature, you inspire others to do the same—and that is a precious gift, because it is the only road to true happiness, peace, and freedom.

Growing up, I tried very hard to be an inoffensive person in order to avoid any further pain or conflict. I strove to be beyond reproach and utterly agreeable, believing that was the easiest way to be loved instead of hurt. But my plan was a complete failure, because subjugating myself to please my parents only made me angry and resentful, and I am certain that my dishonesty about my own needs frustrated my parents.

Though my relationship with both of my parents was challenging and my father was the more perceptibly abusive party, my relationship with my mother was actually more difficult—especially when I started to rebel against the false, meek persona I had created in an effort to be unobjectionable. The complex combustion of her sublimated rage, jealousy, and judgment with my stubbornness, resentment, and desperation to be free created an explosive dynamic.

As a child, I did not understand that our dysfunctional relationship was more complicated than clashing personalities and principles. I later learned that women of my mother's generation grew up while the Divine Feminine—which was exploited, subjugated, and repressed for thousands of years— was still being actively attacked. As a result, they developed survival mechanisms including narcissism, suppression of their true feelings, hostility, and treating other women like adversaries. At present, masculine and feminine energies are being brought back into balance, and the women of my generation—who chose to incarnate onto the earth plane during the great awakening in order to rebalance divine masculinity and femininity—are entirely unwilling to suppress our femininity, confine ourselves to misogynistic standards of acceptability, or hide our true power. This creates a natural and perpetual conflict with previous generations of women and has resulted in many fractured mother-daughter relationships.

Ironically, after shedding old beliefs, false personas, and the need to please or be anyone other than who I am, my relationships are far deeper, more intimate, and more satisfying than they could ever have hoped to be before. You'll notice that the more you raise your vibration, the more you pull others of the same vibration toward you. As you continue to shed trauma and the limiting beliefs it created for you, you'll suddenly find yourself surrounded by your soul tribe, people with whom you feel an intensely strong familial bond, often—as was the case for me—much stronger than the bond your share with your birth families. Upon finding mine, I finally got to experience holidays that truly felt like family celebrations—full of kindness, joy, acceptance, and unconditional love, and absent stress, obligation, tension, and expectation.

So often now, when I host a party for our friends and loved ones, I am awestruck by the incredible camaraderie, gratitude, and genuine appreciation we all have for each other. Sitting around the table basking in the love, light, and laughter of amazing people from all different walks of life truly enjoying each other's company, I can feel the divine in action, and it is an incomparably joyous feeling.

If the suffering of my childhood was the price for the joy I feel and the fun I have with my beautiful family and soul tribe on a daily basis now, it was worth it a thousand times over. Do not compromise yourself to be in a relationship; the future of humanity depends on you being exactly who you are.

## Meditate

Meditation is one of the most effective ways to raise your vibration: it calms your mind, helps you focus on the beauty of the present, and gives you direct access to the divine. Meditation removes the noise and distortion of the outside world and brings you into your sacred heart center, where your true self resides and where you can see and feel everything as it truly is—most importantly, that we are all one, and that separation is an illusion that serves only those who seek to control us.

For many, "meditation" is a scary word and conjures images of people sitting in pretzel-like positions, shifting uncomfortably while they try to shut off all of their thoughts and feelings for hours on end. But this doesn't have to be the case! Meditation does not have to happen in a particular place, position, method, or time; there are no rules. You can (and should) do it anywhere and any way that makes you happy. My favorite way to meditate is to sit on an empty beach, close my eyes, and breathe deeply until I feel complete serenity. I prefer to meditate in nature, because being outdoors naturally raises your vibration, and personally, the ocean brings me great joy and peace. However, there are as many ways to meditate as there are humans on earth. Painting a work of art can be meditative. Listening to gentle music can be meditative. Watching the steam swirl out of a cup of tea can be meditative. You're welcome to go to a meditation class or use a recording to guide you, but it's not necessary. Simply lean up against your favorite tree or relax in the bathtub and practice quieting your mind, being fully present, and letting your energy flow freely.

Meditation is also an excellent time to ask the universe for help. If you are struggling with a relationship, decision, or situation in your life, request assistance; you'll be surprised at how much support you receive. The universe is bountiful, and very often, if you ask for one apple, you'll receive a whole bushel.

## Create, Create, Create!

Many of us—myself included—have raged against injustice, participated in protests, harangued our government officials, and otherwise engaged in battle in an effort to change the dysfunctional systems that are not working for us.

However, this is not the best use of your energy, because it is not possible to change a broken system from within that very system—and continuing to try will only frustrate you, exhaust you, and lower your vibration. Instead, step entirely outside of that broken system and use your energy to create something new. As perfect reflections of the creator, humans have the capacity to be powerful creator beings. Stop participating in the broken paradigms and institutions that are no longer serving you and the collective, and create the world you want to live in.

When school districts shut down during the pandemic, innovative parents all over the country collaborated to create their own schools with educators and curricula that actually support the best interests of children and are free of harmful regulations and nonsensical restrictions. When insurance companies became so greedy and unreliable that they no longer served any benevolent purpose, communities created medical cost-sharing families that pool monthly member dues to cover the health and well-being costs of all members. When countless doctors abandoned their principles during the pandemic and stopped respecting their patients' right to choose what is best for their bodies, pioneering doctors started creating independent health collectives that offer patient-focused health care free of government interference, propaganda, and conflicts of interest.

There is no end to human ingenuity, especially when it comes to creating a better world. If you don't like the way things are, create something new! The limitations our society has convinced us that we have to live within are an illusion; you are a free agent, beholden to none. If you see a better way to do something, bring it into being.

Additionally, embrace the creative expressions your soul craves! Though we are often led to believe that creative pursuits are a waste of time, particularly if they do not generate income, this couldn't be further from the truth. The greatest gift you can give to the world is your most authentic self, so it is absolutely necessary to do the things that bring you joy. At least once daily, make time to create in ways that speak to your soul—write, dance, draw, paint, sing, cook, garden, etc. It is through your authentic creative expression that you contribute your purest self to the world—and that's what you came here to do.

## Trust Your Intuition

Your intuition is your guiding light and most precious gift. The inner voice that tells you what is right or wrong, true or false, is your own higher self's divine wisdom, guiding you along the pathway your soul has chosen.

All too often, our social institutions encourage us to forsake our intuition for what is profitable or otherwise beneficial to them. If you refuse to conform to the unified consciousness of your family, education, religion, or government, and dare to think and act independently, society often labels you as insane or extremist.

However, this is merely social programming designed to prevent you from challenging destructive belief systems, honoring your soul, and exercising your God-given sovereignty. If you allow others to tell you what to think and you acquiesce to values and belief systems that do not resonate with you, you become vulnerable to manipulation—and an easy target for treacherous entities who wish to control you through fear.

Our society has long considered logical-mathematical intelligence to be the most highly prized form of intellect, but we have been duped by those with a vested interest in separating us from our divine instincts. Spiritual and emotional intelligence are the highest, most valuable forms of intellect—and they pose a far greater threat to the forces that wish to retain control over the population.

Your intuition will lead you to the right souls for you, the right places for you, and the right life experiences for you—all in the right timing for you. When you listen to your organic inner knowing, you automatically raise your vibration and align yourself with divine grace and synchronicity. Always, always, always trust your gut.

## Exercise Your Sovereignty

A natural extension of honoring your intuition is exercising your God-given sovereignty. For generations, nefarious governing bodies have tried to convince human beings that they are incapable of making their own choices and thus need to be controlled and dictated to by others. This is patently false; you, and only you, have absolute power over yourself and your actions. You can only be enslaved with your consent. No government, no institution, and no individual has the right to forcibly tell you what to do with your mind, body, or soul. Freedom is the understanding that you have a choice.

At this moment, each of us is being asked to consciously choose a path forward: will you concede to the edicts of a corrupt, greed-based governing body because it is easier to comply than to stand in your own truth, or will you embrace your sovereignty and refuse to participate in a dark agenda you know to be harmful to yourself and others? Every time you make a choice, you are aligning yourself with a system of beliefs and feeding energy into that system—so choose wisely.

Many people are dissatisfied with the world and see the need for change but are waiting for someone in a position of power to create that reality for them while they sit idly by. That is not how it works; no external force can change your experience. Only you can do that. You cast your vote for the experiences you want with your vibration, so you must embody the changes you wish to see in the world.

This is your life and your path, and you are ultimately responsible for your choices, regardless of what a governing body or another person tells you; morality and legality are not the same thing. When the law becomes tyrannical and unjust, it is our obligation to reject it and create new ways of living in a world that works for everyone. In order to create that world, you must be willing to venture beyond the boundaries of comfort and delve into the realm of possibility where the answers await you. Honor yourself by aligning your actions with your intuition and you will naturally raise your vibration and more easily navigate the lessons your soul chose to learn in this lifetime.

## Take Responsibility for Your Energy

You are here to experience having your energy and vibration reflected back to you by others so that you can identify beliefs and behavioral patterns that are no longer serving you and release them. Since you attract what you emit, the world around you acts like a mirror, so if you don't like what you see or experience, it's an invitation to change your energy.

Our latent emotions, behavioral patterns, beliefs, and memories are triggered by others who carry a similar vibration or frequency. In other words, your unresolved emotional experiences act like magnets, attracting others who are carrying the same unresolved emotional baggage. That's why, when you meet someone who is cheerful and upbeat, you often feel joyful and invigorated. When you encounter someone who is angry and withdrawn, you likely respond by becoming grumpy and emotionally unavailable yourself. The goal is to resolve your baggage so that you are free to respond to every person and situation from a place of neutrality, rather than from the same preprogrammed perspective over and over again.

When someone says or does something that subconsciously reminds you of undealt-with trauma, you will respond to that person as if they are the cause of your unhappiness—when in reality, you are responding to a past event that made you feel the same way, which you never dealt with. That unresolved issue constantly gets reactivated by the people around you because your energy is attracting their similar energy. This is why people often get stuck in emotional loops, rehashing past sufferings over and over again and never moving past them.

This is very common in families. When relatives come together for holidays or reunions, no matter how long it has been since they've seen each other, they often fall right back into old behavioral patterns: siblings rehash the same silly childhood battles, parents and children resume old power struggles, and grandparents tell their grown children how to parent. When the presence of family activates old energetic dynamics rooted in trauma, people often regress to the version of themselves that existed at that time.

The way to break this cycle and ensure that you fulfill the journey your soul set out to have is to take responsibility for your energy. Learn to recognize your energetic and emotional patterns, figure out what or who your triggers are, and process out stale energetic residue that is no longer serving you. If you do the work to heal these fragmented parts of yourself, you will shift into an expansive, conscious state of awareness that allows you to see the purpose in everything you have ever experienced—and this is a powerful position indeed.

## Focus on the Positive

Your vibration is determined not only by what you consume and participate in, but also by your focus. Focusing on the positive raises your vibration, while focusing on the negative lowers it. As I learned the hard way by repeatedly attracting the experience of sexual assault, we are electromagnetic beings who attract the same frequencies we emit. So, if you constantly worry about what bad things may befall you, you will actively attract those bad things to you. Contrarily, if you focus on the positive, no matter how small, you will attract good things and raise your vibration. It is your intention and attention—not your mood or emotional state—that creates your vibration.

Since your vibration is determined by your focus—and your response to that focus—it is easy to inadvertently allow your vibration to be dictated by other people, by the news, by your work environment, by world events, or by anything you happen to see, hear, or experience. However, just because your environment offers you something to focus on does not mean you have to accept it; you have a choice. For example, let's say you see a man rob an elderly woman on the street, grabbing her purse and knocking her to the ground in the process. Then, you see a nearby woman run to her aid while her teenage son chases down the purse snatcher. In this situation, you can choose to focus on the injustice of the world, violence against seniors, and your fear of being a victim, or you can choose to focus on the kindness of strangers, the heroism of the boy, and the fact that you are part of a community where people care about one another and come to each other's aid. Neither focus is right or wrong; they simply offer you different experiences. If you focus on the former, you will emit the frequencies of fear, distrust, and sorrow, and attract experiences that support that belief. If you focus on the latter, you will emit the frequencies of love, appreciation, and faith in community, and attract experiences that support that belief. What do you want to experience?

Choosing to focus on the positive does not mean denying that the negative exists. It simply means training your mind to think positively, regardless of your circumstances or external influences. Self-mastery is using your positive focus to create your desired circumstances instead of reacting to the world around you. If you are taking a walk in your new suede shoes and it suddenly starts to pour, don't allow yourself to lament your ruined shoes; focus on how much you love thunderstorms and how every living thing is being quenched and rejuvenated by the healing rain. If the only tickets you can get to a much-anticipated sporting event are in the nosebleed section, don't let yourself mourn how far you are from the action; celebrate the amazing panoramic view and how much easier it is to wrestle your way to the concessions. If you are camping and a hungry bear bulldozes through your campsite and eats all of your food (this one is from personal experience), don't grieve your lost steaks and s'mores; embrace the adventure of foraging through a beautiful forest for your own food . . . or enjoy a good, regenerative fast until you can get to a grocery store. Your focus is always your choice.

When you feel down or depressed, change your focus by immediately doing something to care for yourself. Think of an activity that would improve your mood—perhaps going for a picnic on the beach, snuggling up in front of the fireplace with someone you love, or cooking a truly delectable meal with a dear friend. Stop whatever else you are doing, embrace self-love, and indulge your desires in a healthy, non-addictive way, because unhappiness, depression, and self-loathing all stem from the loss of self that occurs when you do not make self-love a priority. Your most important relationship is with yourself, so keep your vibration high by focusing on what serves your highest, greatest good.

## Lead by Example

Each of us opted to be here on earth at this specific time, on the soul journey of our choosing, to experience the unprecedented awakening of humanity that is taking place. If you are reading this book, you are likely a light worker, a way shower—and you are here to anchor divine love, light, and truth on earth and illuminate the way for all those who come after you.

It is no accident that so many of the angelic warriors at the forefront of this movement come from severely traumatic backgrounds and, in many cases, had to separate from their birth families and the safety net of their belief systems at a young age. By forcing us to deal with our pain and our fears very early, past trauma served as preparation for this moment—and we are now ready to lead.

When you are awake, it can be very difficult to maintain your grace around those who are not—especially when you love them. When people are paralyzed by their fear, they either cannot clearly see what is right, or they see it, but do not have the courage to stand up and act on it. The temptation can be to resort to aggressive tactics and try to "make" them see—but you cannot force someone's eyes open. In fact, those tactics often backfire and drive them further away, or even reinforce their beliefs.

Though it can be frustrating, part of having true faith is realizing that everyone will have the journey they are meant to and awaken in their own divine timing; the process cannot be rushed. Part of our lesson as the awakened is learning to respect that everyone is on their own spiritual path and will reach their destination when they are meant to. This means that we have to lead by example.

Honor the journeys of all others. Allow others to have whatever experiences they wish to have, and do not take their choices personally. You do not have to agree with their choices, but you can never truly know the nature of another's journey, and it is not your right to interfere with it. Besides, when you allow others to be who they are without feeling the need to change them, you free yourself to be who you really are, unburdened of any requirement that someone else change first.

At this moment, there are many people experiencing so much pain that they have lost their connection to love and humanity—and they need your help. Every choice you make and every thought you think vibrates through all of human- ity, causing a ripple effect. So, until those in pain can make loving choices for themselves, do it for them. By being kind, you magnify the vibrations of kindness and make it easier for others to be kind. By being compassionate, you magnify the vibrations of compassion and make it easier for others to be compassionate. By being honest, you magnify the vibrations of honesty and make it easier for others to be honest. Hold up your divine light like a beacon of love and truth and light the path forward for those who cannot yet see.

Though our journey is not yet complete, our destination is preordained—love wins. As my dear, wise friend Christopher said to me, "In the beginning, love is all there ever was, and in the end, love is all that matters." May each of us embody and anchor that divine truth as we work together to create heaven on earth, a beautiful new world that works for all.

# AFTERWORD

## CHRISTOPHER LEE MAHER,
## ADEPT (ARCHITECT OF LIGHT)

Now, THE QUESTION IS what to do and how to do it. But before we get there, let's take some time to recognize the efforts and devotion Brianna has put into developing herself and this incredible, complete work of art. Healing is an art! Everything is a process of co-creation and each moment leads to the next. To let others in on your own shortcomings is a form of leadership I enjoy getting behind, because it encourages me to get a little more raw, a little more open, and a little more transparent about my own journey and continues to manifest and generate greater opportunities to experience greater states of inner freedom and outer peace. Humans are both fragile and mighty. Contrast is how we know where we

are in space and time. Strive to make mistakes and take emotional risks. Share all of your shortcomings with someone you
trust. Every hidden thing inside of you traps your light and
transforms it into a low-cast shadow, but the Light comes for
everyone. Do your best to remember that the most powerful
antidote in the Universe for unrelenting darkness is LOVE.

Sharing one's life experiences—especially those that have
been wrapped in confusion, shame, guilt, anger, betrayal,
abandonment, indifference, and trauma—is quite a vulnerable
thing to do. Transpersonal beings are designed to learn about
life by going into another's story. This entire book is an accom-
plishment from every angle. As you begin to understand the
nature of transpersonal beings, your respect for this form of
delivery will increase. Once you get it, you too will want to
go back and begin again from the beginning of the book and
stand witness to the depth of development necessary for such
a total expression of service.

Being an author myself, I understand and know the process of gathering the courage to let another into my empty,
confused, hurt, anxious, and fearful, shadow-filled spaces. It's
easy to talk about doing, yet difficult to do—at least for me
it was. Opening up and inviting others into the rawness of
human emotions that were overwhelming at the time of those
traumatic events can be healing and can even lead to greater
states of internal freedom and deep inner peace. What you
hold in, stays in, and manifests more heat, pain, confusion,
anxiety, anger, loneliness, and fear. I thank you, Brianna, for

being willing to go so incredibly deep into the impact of those events on a physical, mental, emotional, and energetic/spiritual level.

While reading her words, I laughed, I cried, I cringed, I softened, I related, I emoted, and by the end, I thought, "Oh my goodness, of course this is what life is all about." Taking these multi-generational fear-based states and transforming them into Universal Love-based states seems like an enormous duty, and yet the reward is so much greater than the efforts expressed. What of value would any of us do without love?

The Universe is always conspiring to my and your benefit. The answer is so simple: reduce your shadow and simultaneously amplify your light. Take a tiny (or big) step every day, and soon enough you are *free* to choose the life you really want—a life you know is meant for you, as opposed to becoming a slightly different version of Mom and Dad. How will you know who you really are without taking any risks? Your mind is a tiny grain of sand and your heart has access to all the sand in the universe, which begs the question, "Where do I put my focus?" And the answer, as Brianna laid out for you, is on all of it: look under every stone, pebble, leaf, and fallen tree in the forest of your collective experience. Your triggers are your keys to freedom and peace. Be grateful for those who set you off because they are showing you where your beliefs compete with reality, and where conscious investigation and healing are needed.

From my perspective, our world is in deep need of leaders like this author, who are willing to give us examples of intense emotional honesty. There is a quiet sage in every one of us who is looking and waiting for their moment. That moment is now. Reach deep within and call with clear intent the light-hearted, focused souls who can help you make straight again that which was made crooked generations before you were born.

The world is open to listening, learning, and feeling from those whose only intent is to serve powerfully. This is the time to take a risk. We all need to know and make sense of the depth of impact these types of trauma events have and have had on every aspect of our beings. Once this is known and understood fully, we can begin to take steps to heal, repair, integrate, and make whole again that which has been fragmented, broken, and frayed. What else is more worthy of your attention, of your affection, of your focus, of your devotion, of your understanding, of your love? If you agree and are nodding your head, then go back through the book and all of its suggestions, identify which one feels most vulnerable for you, and begin there; that would be the prudent thing to do. Your time is now and this window's opening may be short.

The Reclamation of Light is the pathway out of Darkness, and now that you know that it is 1,000 percent possible, what are you waiting for? Without transmutation and transfiguration, humanity will continue to wade through quicksand; consciousness is key. As an Adept (Architect of Light), I hold the seven keys for True Transformation and wield the Royal Blue Flame Ray of Light and the Silver Flame Ray of Light.

Find me and learn how to grow beyond the limitations of your mind so you can project from your heart. This portal of Light rebukes and transmutes the greatest levels of shadow and darkness known to mankind. Reclaiming your light is meant to be easy, instantaneous, and permanent. You deserve to feel free, be happy, and live in peace, so summon the courage to find your way back home. A quiet mind, comfortable body, grounded yet excitable emotions, and endless amounts of energy are your birthright—but you have to go get it. Again, what are you waiting for? You are ready for your mystical life. I can feel it. Go all in. Remember, no risk it, no biscuit . . .